M000282163

Healing Tree

To My Dearest JinHee Nim,
I am so grateful to have
you as part of my HongIk family
here in WA. I am forever
thankful for your love &
light ☀️

love,
Johwatong

Healing Tree

An Adoptee's Story about
Hurting, Healing, and Letting the
Light Shine Through

DANIELLE GAUDETTE

healingtree
publishing

SEATTLE, WASHINGTON

healingtree publishing

Seattle, Washington

Copyright © 2022 by Danielle Gaudette. All rights reserved.

Cataloging-in-Publication Data is on file with the Library of Congress

Paperback ISBN: 9780578351544

eBook ISBN: 9780578351551

Book cover and interior design by Christina Thiele

Editorial production by kn literary

daniellegaudette.com

Printed in the United States of America

To my two mothers and my two fathers,
with gratitude

Contents

PART TWO

Introduction

Thank you for opening this book. It's a book about my world—my inner world, mostly. It's a book about hope.

I decided to write it because I had found my inner world to be a complicated place that challenged me throughout much of my life, but one that eventually brought me to discover great possibility within.

Why I struggled so much, I cannot say. I don't believe it is something I can know for certain, nor is it any longer relevant to my healing journey to know the why of it. What I choose to *do* about this suffering has now become what is important to me.

I have learned that our suffering can be useful—provided we find a constructive way to share it. In letting others know how we face and process our own suffering, those who also suffer may feel less alone. It is my hope that communicating my own journey, as one adoptee navigating this life, may somehow help you, my fellow adoptees, in navigating yours.

It is never easy to peer into the dark corners of our minds in order to gain clarity. Since I found myself with no choice but to spend considerable time peering into mine, I wanted my discoveries to be useful for as many people as possible. At the very least, what I have learned may just comfort you to know that you are not the only one who feels what you feel and to remind you that there is always light, not too far from your reach, no matter how black it gets.

Maybe you are not an adoptee, but you have an adoptee in your life and sometimes find yourself puzzled by his or her behaviors. I hope the revealing of parts of my own psyche will provide you some insight.

Perhaps you are not an adoptee, nor do you know any adoptees; nevertheless, you find yourself holding this book. For you, I hope the honest expression of my heart and soul, as well as the self-development tools I present, may assist you on your own personal path of healing and growth.

In Part One, I have put together glimpses of my adopted life, of reuniting with my birth mother when I was twenty-one years old, and of how my path toward healing began. I share those personal experiences from where they live in the deepest parts of my heart and mind.

In Part Two, I introduce you to principles and practices vital to my healing process. When I found the practice of Body & Brain, I was very much in need of healing as my mind was coming apart, my heart was hurting, and my spirit was in darkness. To reclaim my sense of self and to recover my spirit, I became a practitioner and, in time, a trainer of these methods. I have been sharing what I have learned with students across the country for the last twenty years.

Not only did I want to lay out for you my own human journey, my human suffering, but I also wanted to provide hopeful tools and specific practices for others who may find themselves with similar struggles—tools I use to work through challenges I still face today. For, no matter how diligently I have been dedicated to my own healing process, I have discovered there is always more space for reconciliation within myself and with others. There is always more forgiveness to grant, more acceptance to embrace, more love to be realized.

My wish is that you who have found this book will sit with me for an honest exploration of the inner world. I hope that in my divulging both the agonies and the possibilities that I have found within, my story and my offerings will lend you strength, clarity, and wisdom as you navigate your own unique and precious healing journey.

Part One

"The wound is the place where the light enters you."

—Rumi

The Tree in Me

*T*housands of twinkling stars filled my senses as I eagerly made my way down the gravel pathway. I could feel the energy of the desert—clear, almost electric. Mountains of red rock surrounding the Sedona Mago Center seemed to be watching me move through the quiet night. I hurried past the casitas where other retreat-goers rested, my mind and body practically buzzing. I was heading to my first-ever spiritual healing session.

A warm-spirited Korean woman welcomed me into a dimly lit, quiet space. The room was modestly adorned with an Asian screen and a large healing mat on the floor. She guided me to remove my shoes and lie down on the mat. Nervous, as I always was, I lay down on my back and tried to relax.

The woman, a master energy healer, sat down beside me and, starting at the top of my head, scanned my body with her hands. As she did so, she began to speak in a gentle, curious voice that sounded like she was pondering a mystery. "Hmmm . . . Your energy is so blocked," she said. "Why so blocked like this? You're a young girl. Why is your energy so heavy and blocked? It doesn't flow like water. It's like dark yellow jelly."

At that time, I had very little awareness of myself, of what was going on inside me, or of what she was really talking about.

I was twenty-three years old, and all I knew was that I was not happy. More accurately, although I was the happiest I had been in years, I was nevertheless overwrought with anxiety, worry, and fear. I now know that those feelings were just a tiny fragment of the teeming mass that lay within me.

The healer continued to scan me—my brain, my chest, my abdomen—and when she finally waved her hand over the right side of my belly, the area over my liver and right kidney, she said, "Tell me about your mother."

To this day, I don't know which mother she was talking about. There was the possibility that she could have meant my biological mother whom I had met for the first time two years prior. I sometimes wonder how the session would have gone had I named her. But she was not the one who came to mind. At that moment, I only wanted to tell the healer how my mother had struggled severely with mental illness ever since I was five years old, how painful that was for me, and how much I worried about her day and night. I wanted to tell her how I had made trying to help my mother my full-time job for as long as I could remember, but no matter how much I tried, I couldn't help her, I couldn't change her. That's what I wanted to say.

To my surprise, all that came out of my mouth was, "She's so sick."

Before I could continue, I burst into tears. It was an unexpected, massive explosion that seemed to shoot out from my entire being. As I shook and wailed at the top of my lungs, I felt like every organ and cell was sobbing. It was as if someone had opened a hole on the top of my head and turned on a fire hose.

A strong current of energy coursed through my body, pushing out so much hurt, so much fear and sadness, anger and grief from every hidden corner of me. All the while, the Korean woman kept saying softly, "Good, very good. Very good job, keeeeep going . . ."

There was a monsoon inside of me that day—a physical, energetic, and spiritual monsoon. After the storm had finally calmed, the energy healer said to me, "You had taken all your mother's illness into your body. That's how much you wanted to help her, but you, yourself, were being poisoned. Now, new life is being restored inside your body. Breathe it in. Now, your tears are changing into tears of gratitude. Feel the new life growing inside of you."

That's when I saw—no, not just saw, I *felt*—a giant tree growing through my body. Its massive roots spiraled down my legs. The place of great power where the roots and trunk connected was in the area of my lower abdomen, my second chakra. I felt amazing strength. The thick trunk grew up and quickly spread out into branches of fresh green leaves, stretching their arms through me. Behind the branches, the bright sun shone through in the place of my heart chakra, the very center of my chest, filling me with golden light. My tears, once a storm of emotion, softened. I felt alive, truly alive. The freedom and power of Life itself was born inside of me as a Healing Tree.

When the session was over, I was unable to speak. I could hardly remember how to tie my sneakers, as I felt completely new. Gentle tears continued to flow as I bowed to thank my healer. Reaching for the door to usher me out, she spoke to me one more time, assuring me, "Once your mother's pain has fully left you, your tears will turn to laughter."

Next morning at breakfast, I met up with some friends from my retreat who asked me to share my experience with the energy healer. I opened my mouth to explain, but there were still no words. Instead, I began to laugh. I laughed and laughed and laughed. I didn't understand why, but it was joyous and refreshing. My compassionate friends rubbed my back and held my hand. They could feel that something healing and transformative, beyond any description, had happened to me.

In the days that followed, I felt a quiet and a clarity I had never known. The birds chirped more pleasantly, and even the tiny white wildflowers on the side of the road appeared more vibrant. I had experienced an energetic purging of the emotional pain I had been holding on to for a lifetime. I was clean and light and free.

Though I didn't know it then, such a complete letting go cleansed so much of the agony of my childhood that it made room for a deeper wound to rise to the surface to be healed. That wound—my first wound in this life—was deeply hidden from my awareness and etched profoundly into my psyche. It would take time and an immense amount of practice before I was strong enough to even see it, let alone take it on.

The universe only gives us what we are ready for, when we are ready for it. For that glorious summer of 2000, I was ready to enjoy the peaceful, healing respite the universe had gifted me.

Sun between the Branches

I have always loved trees.

As a child, I played with them, building worlds under their branches, worlds filled with my imaginary friends—Amy, Robbie, Johnny, and Stephanie, to name a few. Trees became our houses, our hangouts, our local neighborhood market. Their shady spaces allowed me to do and be whatever I dreamed.

As a teenager, just being near trees was soothing for me. It was as if I could *feel* each tree, its presence breathing inside. Awakening to the fact that there was a force of life bursting from each tree, I felt compelled to communicate with it. I sometimes liked to press my cheek against a big maple leaf, or squat down to feel life pulsing through thick roots as they plunged into the soil.

As a college student, whenever I felt lost, misunderstood, or alone, or when I couldn't find my place among my peers, I would just like to be near trees. Walking by them, writing a poem underneath them, or leaning my head against their comforting, quiet strength, I would feel the support of their almost-holy presence. I would feel somehow understood, embraced.

Such solace meant so much to me because I had a constant feeling of not belonging—of not being, feeling, thinking like my peers—of not wanting to do what they wanted to do. I tried to go to parties, but I always felt empty and bored and would slip out when no one was paying attention. I tried to listen to classmates urging me to get involved with women's rights, climate change, or the latest antiwar efforts. Although I cared deeply about humanity and the earth, I couldn't resonate with what they were saying. I felt only their anger and judgment, which left me feeling even more separated and confused. Being human felt like such a strenuous task. The world frightened me, and I couldn't find a place to rest my mind.

When I was overwhelmed by it all, when I didn't want to be a human, I would sometimes think I wanted to *be* a tree. I, too, wanted to dip my toes deep into the soil and drink from the cool, wet earth. I, too, wanted to reach my arms and my fingertips up to the sky, brave branches reaching toward the sun, leaves stirring in the breeze. I longed to feel the air, the rain, the wind, the sunshine. I felt it would be so healing, so peaceful, so liberating to just be.

During my first spiritual healing session in Sedona, my wish had come true. For just a few precious, unforgettable moments, I got to *be* a tree! I became as intimately connected to the Healing Tree within me as I was to the trees outside of me. My inner Healing Tree took on the symbol of my healing journey. Her roots encouraged me to be strong, and the sun between her branches encouraged me to be bright. Her message was to heal, to infuse her healing spirit into my daily life.

Shortly after returning from Sedona, inspired by my awakening, I wrote this poem:

Sun Between the Branches

Her voice is sandy like mustard when she laughs, and she is laughing her way to enlightenment, she says.

She is sun between the branches on her best day, and every day other, whether she remembers it or not.

She knows this at 6 a.m. morning-blossom bike ride, as her cold fingers grip handlebars, and she chases the last of the full moon falling behind the trees.

"Don't judge," she hears a voice say. She knows it is that of the moon, who ceaselessly teaches her eternal love—love with no conditions, no judgments.

And suddenly, everything is as simple as this.

Her Soul smiles new-day sunlight between the branches, and her hips shudder with the power of tree roots. She is the strength she needs to go on, and she is filled with a message of light: love and heal.

And this is all she needs at 6 a.m. morning glory or on any day, ever.

"I will do my job," she promises, as the moon and trees do, and the blue-sky sun-filled day.

I will do my job.

My Mother

Beverly Marie Gaudette
October 19, 1948–December 16, 2013

She was the only mother I knew for the first twenty-one years of my life. She is the one who mothered me through my every moment. So, if you ask me, "Who is your *real* mother?" I will tell you, "She is."

I remember writing her long love letters, when I was little, about how I felt we were one, stuck together like glue, that I was she and she was me. Even as a teenager, I told her all my secrets, all my gossip, and she was there for me through every single drama, wiping away my tears and reminding me that I was perfect. When it came to love, she held nothing back. When it came to laughter, it was her deep belly laugh that left us howling on the bed, in the car, or on the kitchen floor.

As I grew into adulthood, my mother trusted me and supported me in all my choices, even the ones that were difficult for her to accept. If she knew there was something I truly wanted, she put her own ideas and expectations aside and just embraced me. She led my father, a gentle and kind man, to do the same. Back then, I didn't realize how rare and precious it was to have my parents always on my side. What I did know is that, in turn, they had my full trust and loyalty.

However, the sharp thorn that pierced my heart was my mother's suffering from horrible and often debilitating bouts of severe anxiety and depression. This mental illness was her adult way of trying to process the sexual abuse she had experienced when she was eight years old. It haunted her life—our lives—and sent her down a dark road of endless psychotherapy, heavy medications, and two separate rounds of electroshock treatment. It was a mental illness that, I believe, led to her untimely death.

Her pain was my pain. I did everything I could to try to make her happy. I danced, I sang, I staged shows on the living room floor. I would drag Renée, my younger sister, out of bed early on Saturday mornings for a performance. Over her sleepy face and her little purple pajama set, I'd dress her up in a miscellaneous collection of threadbare, oversized hats, scarves, and mittens—anything I could find in my parents' coat closet. Then, I would get my mother and father out of bed and sit them down on the couch for front row seats. Although poor Renée was confused and miserable, to me, it was all worth it, as long as it made my mother laugh.

I poured my heart and soul into her well-being for fifteen hardworking years of my young life. Although she loved me infinitely and would do anything for me, there was one thing she couldn't do for me: heal herself.

Ultimately, my mother suffered a hemorrhagic stroke and, per the doctor, "incurred multiple infarctions." Although she survived, she was left with severe brain damage. A top neurologist at Boston's Beth Israel Hospital explained to us that her brain had been damaged in ten different places, and because of that, it looked like the brain of a person with advanced dementia. She was sixty-one years old; I was thirty-three.

From that day, until the day of her death three-and-a-half years later, she languished in a bed, slowly withering away. She never recovered her ability to articulate what was going on inside her, nor was she able to comprehend what was going on in the world around her. In her final year of life, she barely communicated at all. She took in food through a tube that had been surgically placed into her stomach during her initial emergency brain surgery. The tube was never removed. She had no quality of life, and watching her live that way was torturing the hearts of those who loved her.

Every time I visited her, I felt ill the moment I stepped into the elevator. Walking down the long hallway to her room, I held my breath because I didn't want to smell the odor of people who were neither alive nor dead. I didn't want the reminder that my mother was in such a place. Wingate was considered a nursing home for patients who required tubes and drips but who weren't eligible to stay at the hospital because they no longer had the possibility of getting better. To me, it was purgatory for the living.

Once in my mother's room, I would still smile as I sang to her, rubbed her hair, and asked her questions to try to get a nod or a grin out of her. I felt more comfortable there than in the hallways. Flowers, plants, and Hallmark cards lined the windowsill. To make the space more homey, my father had hung family photos next to her bed and brought in a CD player so she could listen to her favorite music. While the atmosphere he created helped me to relax a bit, my heart always sank when, as I stepped into the elevator on my way out, I would see the plaque stating that this long-term care facility was, basically, a hospice.

As hard as it was to be losing my mother, I felt a certain degree of contentment. My fourteen years of spiritual practice and healing had prepared me for this moment that would have once been nearly impossible to handle. I knew I had done my very best for my mother in this life, and all I wanted was for her suffering to come to an end.

In the moment she left this world, I was sitting in a chair by her bed. My father was there, along with Renée, my aunt Gail, and my cousin Carly. We had been taking turns by her bedside for ten days, since we knew they were her last.

Suddenly, there was a strong and bright energy all around me, and I felt my mother's spirit escape from her shriveled body. That spirit was big and joyous, and it was somersaulting around the room, celebrating its freedom. Renée cried out in grief and ran into the hallway; my father put his arms around my aunt and my cousin who were standing near him; I just sat clutching the center of my exploding chest. Tears mixed with grief and gratitude, joy and awe, streamed down my cheeks. I realized, at that moment, that my mother was not an unfortunate, pitiful, mentally ill person who had suffered deeply for most of her life. That's not who she was at all! She was a great spirit who had come to this life to experience something she *needed* to experience, something that, on some level, she actually *wanted* to experience. I felt her true spirit—beyond the brain-damaged woman she had been for years, beyond the sickness and the suffering of her life—a spirit filled with love and a kind of bronze, warm, sandy light. I wasn't aware of it before, but it was clear now that this was the light I had always seen in her hazel eyes. It was the light of her smile that filled a room. This was, and always had been, her unbreakable spirit shining through. It was a spirit that soothed me and healed me in so many ways throughout my life, a spirit that I was honored to love and be loved by, a spirit I had missed during the long years after her brain had been broken, but it was right there before me on that day, dazzling me with her brilliant good-bye.

Angel-Heart Queen

(1998—written for my mother when I was twenty-two years old, right before graduating from college)

There is a woman I know
whose heart is filled with angels.
Infinite numbers.
They sing when she speaks,
and when she smiles,
they fly out into the world.
Tiny white-winged angels of love
encircle me.
I have known this woman
my whole life,
and longer, I sometimes feel.
Perhaps I was her mother in another world,
and she mine, before that,

and she mine, now.
The circle is endless.
She is the angel-heart queen of my world.
Now,
always.
If she could know
that sometimes
when I sleep,
when I walk,
when I breathe,
I cry.
Tiny white-winged angels of love multiply
across distances
and enter me.
They flow through me,
every cell of my body,
every capillary of my soul,
and exit me,
through tears.
Perhaps they fly back to her
and whisper my love,
recycled,
reborn.
Holy is the angel-heart queen.
And my love too.
(I miss you.)

My Mother's Bed

(2000—written when I was twenty-four years old, shortly after my healing session in Sedona)

She wants to burn her mother's bed.

Bed of sickness and sorrow

Bed of fearful nervous heart

Bed of poor me why God why? Help me please O God I can't take another day.

Bed of no will

Bed of hopelessness

Bed of soul dying.

She wants to burn her mother's bed.

Then. She changes. Her mind.

There is stillness all around them, she imagines, in the quiet hours of a 4 a.m. new day.

Now, there is a yellow rose in her heart, and she sends a rainbow message to her mother's yellow rose.

"Come out, come out, wherever you are!" she whispers. And waits.

They become surrounded by capsules of white light.

There is a rainbow bridge connecting them.

And she asks that the capsule become an ocean of light to cleanse her mother's body.

Out! Out! with the dirty seaweed sadness in rippling waves.

Residue, like thick mud, builds up and oozes from her mother's fingertips and toes, and daughter cleans it up with tears of gratitude.

This is healing.

The message comes clear like a song she suddenly remembers: Love and Heal. Love and Heal. This is all she wants to do.

The apple tree in her yard tells her there is fruit in her heart, and her mother is her student, and her mother is her teacher.

And the whole world is waiting.

Sunlight shines through branches.

And she knows that this is Life.

Simple.

So, she changes her mind, one day.

This is the story of a girl who changed her mind.

One day.

Bed of hope and healing

Bed of restoration

Bed of noonday naptime, sunshine seeping through

And laughter, like butterflies, all around us.

You Did It

(2013—written when I was thirty-six years old, just before my mother's passing)

My Mother,

my Angel-Heart Queen,

you taught me how to love. You taught me how to laugh. You saved my life.

You did it.

My Mother,

my Angel-Heart Queen,

you embraced two abandoned little girls.

You made them feel like the most adored and special little people on planet Earth.

You did the most important thing that any one human could do.

You completed your work.

You did an amazing job.

You did it.

My Mother,

my Angel-Heart Queen,

you suffered enough.

You endured endless hurt and pain. The darkest suffering—you persevered again. And again. In the name of Love.

You did it.

My Mother,

my Angel-Heart Queen,

you suffered enough.

You paid back your debts.

You cleaned up your karma.

You did it.

My Mother,

my Angel-Heart Queen,

you're done. You're finished. You don't have to suffer anymore. No more.

Do you hear me?

Please hear me.

I promise you . . .

There is more Joy than this, waiting for you.

There is more Light than this, waiting for you.

There is more Peace than this, waiting for you.

It's your time now.

Time to be free.

Time for peace—finally.

Our Mother.

Our Angel-Heart Queen.

Our Savior, our Hero, our Friend.

You will live forever in our hearts.

And we will meet again soon,

in a happier place than this.

We want to see you smile again.

So, go.

You're done.

You did it.

You're free.

Our Angel-Heart Queen.

It's time to go back to Heaven.

I will sing for you,

and you can fly.

I Was Adopted

When I tell people I was adopted, they usually ask me, "When did you find out?" I cannot pinpoint one particular moment when that happened; I feel like I always knew. When I was very small, my mother used to say, "You didn't grow in my belly. You grew in another lady's belly, and then we came to get you. You are our adopted angel."

I remember her telling me that story before I was in school or even old enough to realize that this was something that made me different. From the time I was small enough to walk through my father's legs as he made a tunnel for me, or ride on his back while he "horseyed" around the house, I knew where I had come from. Because my parents loved me with what I now feel was a rare and unconditional love, I accepted whatever they told me with an open heart and without a single question. I felt good about being their adopted angel. I cherished the way my dad slow danced on his knees with me to Billy Joel's "Honesty," and the way my mom rubbed my hair and cheeks, infusing me with her love, professing my perfection.

Even when they told the tale of my adoption, they made me feel special. It was a tale I heard time and again, and it goes like this:

My parents desperately wanted to have a baby, but, for some unclear reason, my mother was unable to get pregnant. So they put their names on a list to adopt a baby, but the expected wait time for an adoption in Massachusetts was four years. Their hearts were aching.

Wanting to help, my mother's cousin and his wife introduced my parents to friends who had connections with Cardinal Cooke, the church official who oversaw the Catholic Charities in Manhattan. They asked him to help my parents find a child to adopt in the state of New York. Through him, my parents met Sister Una McCormack, the executive director of the Catholic Home Bureau. In ten short months, it was she who was able to find them a baby to adopt—in New York City. My parents were beside themselves with joy, feeling that a great blessing had come to them.

They drove four hours to Manhattan to get me. My grandfather was at the wheel, my grandmother beside him, and my parents in the back seat with a pillow upon which they could hardly wait to rest me.

Once at Catholic Charities, my mother and father were led into a big room with a big mirror, and in the middle of that room was a big crib. Unbeknownst to them, the mirror was two-way. Behind it, nurses gathered to observe the parents' authentic reactions when they saw the baby for the first time. Should they detect a lack of warmth or connection from the parents, the nurses had the right to recommend that the adoption process be discontinued.

My parents crept up to the crib and peered over the bars.

There they found the "tiniest peanut" with a bush of black hair, lying quietly, waiting for them on her tenth day of life. My mother's heart leapt with happiness that her prayers had been answered, and she burst into tears. She threw her arms around my father, who, always the soul of stability and reason, was now beside himself with glee, and the two of them started jumping up and down. Unable to contain the depth of her joy, my mother hopped onto my father's back. Spurred on by the moment, he galloped around the room with my mother in a piggyback ride of sheer bliss, both of them cheering and crying and laughing.

Behind the mirror, the nurses were so heart-warmed that they, too, began to cry and hug each other. Everyone was ushered into the room to celebrate, including my grandparents. One nurse approached my mother and said, "I have never seen such a connection and display of love. I would like to arrange for you to bring your baby to the archbishop to receive his blessing." So, she did. From that moment on, I became their "blessed little adopted angel."

As they had planned, I rode back to Massachusetts on a pillow. Because my grandfather kept looking over his shoulder to admire me, we almost got into an accident on I-95. We had to pull off the highway so my father could take the wheel, and my grandfather could have his chance to get in on the cuddling. It was a celebratory day for everyone, so much so that when my father turned the corner onto our street in Watertown, they were surprised to find the *entire street* lined with lawn chairs filled with family, friends, and neighbors, all waiting to greet me.

Our street, Piermont Street, had once been part of my

grandfather's family farm. His parents, who had come over from Italy, had raised their large family of seven children in the big white house on the corner. When they grew older, my grandfather and his brothers built houses, including our duplex, and turned their farm into the beginnings of a suburban neighborhood. My mother, part of this large Italian family, knew many people throughout town, and I think they were *all* there to greet me that day!

Her cousin Sandy, a schoolteacher, worked together with her third-grade students to create a welcome-to-my-new-home banner for me. It was handmade with magic markers on bright yellow construction paper and was hung by neighbors above the garage of our apartment. It read: "Welcome, Baby Danielle."

This is my rendition of the sweet story I grew up listening to, a story that warms my heart, even now, as I write it; it is the story of a baby who got a lucky break. It's not easy to be "unwanted" by the people who created you, but on the tenth day of my existence, I became the most wanted and highly celebrated little creature in my own small piece of the universe—loved, adored, and deeply cherished.

I am very blessed—it's true. My parents were honest, wholesome people. My mother showed me how to love and be loved. My father showed me how to be stable, loyal, and how to keep a pure heart—to feed the ducks, squirrels, and stray cats of the world; to take pictures of beautiful flowers and butterflies; and to always look up and appreciate the moon. The foundation they laid for me at the beginning of my life was critical in allowing me to be who I am today, and I am deeply grateful.

Née

our years later, the Massachusetts waiting list had finally run its course, a baby was ready for us, and we adopted my sister, Renée.

Renée's story was different from mine. She was eight months old and had been living with a foster family. The family had called her Leslie, but my father wanted to give her a French name, as he had given me. Just like my parents had received information that my birth mother had given me up for adoption because she was pursuing her acting career, they were told that Renée's biological mother was sixteen years old when she gave birth, that she did not know who the father was, and that she never wanted to be contacted.

I was allowed to go with my parents and grandparents into downtown Boston on the day we picked her up. I remember playing with a massive dollhouse in the waiting room. The dolls were bendy and unfamiliar compared to my collection of Barbies. My mother used to say I could play with them for hours and not make a peep. I always found my dolls and imaginary friends to be much more interesting than other children were, as I could create my own world with them—the world that *I* wanted. However, I did long to have a real, live, baby sister of my own to play with.

I felt quiet inside while I waited for her. Eventually, a woman came in and asked me if I'd like to help dress my new baby sister. We walked down a long hallway into a room where another woman was getting the baby ready. Little Née was lying on a table. She had soft, pale skin, a perfectly pink button nose, and glistening eyelashes that showed she had been crying. She was wearing an oversized, fire-engine red snowsuit that was literally hanging off her legs. It seemed odd to me that someone would put something so big on her, and it was clear to me that she needed a much more suitable outfit. I stood there "helping" (watching) the ladies put her into a little white dress that my mother had brought, followed by a light-yellow snowsuit that fit her perfectly. Then, she was ready. Ready for what? Ready to become part of the Gaudette family.

We walked back down the long hallway to take Renée to my parents. I don't think I understood enough about what was going on to feel the joy or the butterflies or whatever other feeling might have been in order. Within minutes of the woman handing Renée over to my mother, though, it became clear to me that I was no longer the only "little adopted angel" of the family. Although my inner princess was jarred by this, once I realized that I still got to be in the photographs, I decided to share the limelight.

I loved my little sister very much, yet soon after we got her home, I discovered that we were two entirely different peas living in the same pod. One morning I was trying to play with her while my mother was on the phone. I was crawling around the house beside her, getting in her face to talk baby talk, when she whapped me over the head with her bottle. I was shocked! No one had ever done such a thing to me before. Not long after that, she was sitting in her high chair, and, as an act of great honor, I allowed her to hold my dearly beloved Cabbage Patch Kid. I thought I might win her heart with my generous gesture, but it meant nothing to her. She just chucked that doll away. Its poor plastic face hit the kitchen floor with a devastating smack. I was starting to get the impression that perhaps we didn't have a lot in common.

I was right.

Growing up, while I was playing with imaginary friends, putting on shows, reading, and writing poetry, Renée was outside riding her bike, playing kickball, and bossing around all the boys on the block. I wasn't one for playing much with other kids, except for my older cousin Carly. She was my bestie, and we had all sorts of adventures with Barbie dolls and jelly shoes and raiding my mother's lingerie drawer for dress-up. Renée, on the other hand, preferred to run around the yard, hitting, kicking, and throwing any kind of ball she could get her hands on—cheering, booing, and hooting sports-like noises for hours with her buddies. She had a large posse of friends, at least one of them always right by her side, "attached to her hip," as my mother would say.

As I got older, I always felt she was the lucky one because, whenever my mother had one of her Sunday morning nervous breakdowns, Renée got to take off with her friends. She was younger, and my father allowed her to go. I was the one who had to stay behind, be responsible, and help him bring the situation back to some degree of normalcy. I was the one who had to sit down on the kitchen floor where my mother had collapsed into a pile of trembling tears, put her head on my lap, rub her hair, and promise her that everything was okay. I did it willingly, time and again, because I loved my mother infinitely and I wanted to help my family, but, over time, I grew resentful of my overwhelming responsibility.

Once I reached adolescence, I began to take out my anger on Renée. I chased her and hit her far more often than I would like to admit. One time I even threw the telephone at her. I teased her so mercilessly about her toes, saying they looked like Fred Flintstone's, that for years she wouldn't take her socks off, even when we sat by the swimming pool. She was a tomboy, and I was a wimp, so I didn't have a chance against her in a real fight, but when I was angry, I was mean. She needed my love, but I didn't give it to her. That was my biggest crime against her. I was supposed to be her big sister and her protector, but I failed to play that role.

There we were, two little adoptees trying to figure out what the heck life was all about on Piermont Street—she in her way, I in mine. Whether we had things in common or not, whether we got along or not, she was my sister, through and through, my only sibling. She lived, and still lives, in that special place in my heart. Although we were not bound by blood, we were bound by childhood. We share the same memories of the same family, of *our* family: memories of my mother's famous mashed potatoes, my father's bad jokes, and my teaching her how to do multiplication and division before she had even gone to kindergarten; memories of how she hoarded Reese's Peanut Butter Cups under her bed, and how I snuck boys into the house on those hot summer days when my parents were still at work; memories I have that only she knows, because only she was right there with me.

That is our sisterhood. That is our love.

Finding Them

I was curious. It wasn't a curiosity that haunted me, but from time to time, I would wonder: Where did this face come from? Where did this body come from? Where did this *blood* come from?

I knew when I turned eighteen, I would be eligible to begin the search for my biological parents. Although my mother and father neither encouraged nor discouraged such a search, they had always made it clear that, when the time came, the choice was available to me if I wanted to make it.

My eighteenth year came and went. I was in the thick of my senior year of high school, choosing colleges and planning to leave home for the first time.

Separating from my parents was tough for all of us. Standing outside my dormitory at the University of New Hampshire, I hugged my mother so tightly, and for so long, that my tears streamed all over the collar of her suede jacket. I wanted to feel her love and drink in the scent of her perfume as much as I possibly could until I saw her again. Tears streaked her makeup as she watched me wrap my arms around my father, pressing my wet cheek into his chest, thanking him for being the best daddy in the whole world. I was still sobbing as they walked away hand in hand—as they always did. Later, my father shared with me that on the ride home, my mother was crying so hard she made him pull over on the side of the highway so she could throw up.

My freshman year led me down a rabbit hole. Had I just smoked marijuana every day and dropped acid on the weekends, I may have fit in better. I would get into my pajamas on Friday after my last class and not get out of them until Monday morning, hiding in my dorm room, writing short stories and working on my novella. Searching for my biological parents was the furthest thing from my mind. It wasn't until I transferred to the University of Iowa in my sophomore year, settling into my study of creative writing and preparing for a semester abroad, that my curiosity swelled.

Persistent questions from friends started to get to me: "Where are you from originally?" "What's your heritage?" Of course I couldn't answer because I didn't know. Then they would have fun guessing: "Italian!" "French!" "Native American!" "Polynesian!" I heard it all, yet I had no idea. *If I could just get a couple of pictures and some information about the people who created me,* I thought, *then I'll be able to fill in a missing piece about myself.* That was all I set out to look for—a couple of pictures and some information. That would suffice. The thought of wanting to *know* these people, or have some kind of *relationship* with them, was so unsettling to me. It seemed complicated and stressful. I already had my mother and father, my world. I didn't want to rock that boat. I was confident about my parents. I was just dissatisfied with the missing piece: Where on earth had I come from?

Not having answers to the questions others grew up knowing—about their father's long Italian nose, or their mother's sun-kissed Columbian skin—set me apart. It reminded me that I was somehow different from the average person.

I had awakened to that difference when I was in second grade. We were in the library for story time, and the librarian explained to us that the book she had just read was "adapted" by such-and-such a person.

"Like me! I was adapted!" I declared, raising my hand proudly.

"Yes, Danielle, I believe you mean to say that you were *adopted*." She smiled.

I nodded with confidence.

When we got back to our desks, I was mortified when my friends gathered around me, telling me they didn't believe me. Had I said something strange? Until that moment, being adopted was normal to me. In fact, in my family, being adopted was special. The angel-princess in me was pained to realize that there was suddenly something *so* unusual about me that it had shocked my classmates into disbelief. My heart sank when a small group of them followed me to my mother's car after school to ask her if it was really true.

"Yes," she told them warmly, "it is."

As she assured them and helped me into the car, I felt her concern for me. I was devastated to recognize, for the first time, that on a social level, being adopted made me different.

So, in the fall of 1997, in the tiny shoebox of a room I was renting in a creaky old house in Iowa City, I sat down to write a letter to Catholic Charities. It stated who I was and that I was interested in finding out more information about my biological parents. To my surprise, I received a response almost right away.

It said that all my files had burned in a fire and that I would have to write to the state of New York for further information. *Oh, great,* I thought. *Now I'm Orphan Annie!*

Nonetheless, I wrote a letter to the state of New York and sent it off right before I left for Ireland to study abroad for a semester. Strategically, I put my parents' home as the return address because I would be spending the summer in Boston once I got back to the States. As I stuffed my letter in the mailbox, I figured I would just check on it after my James Joyce-reading, pub-crawling, Guinness-drinking, hitchhiking, twenty-first birthday-celebrating adventure on the Emerald Isle.

The Phone Call

*A*s planned, I returned to Watertown for the summer of 1998 to stay with my parents until school started again. One morning, while I was sitting at the kitchen table, eating a bowl of Cheerios, the letter popped back into my mind.

"Hey, Daddy, did I get any mail from the state of New York while I was gone?"

My father, the rock-solid, reliable, keeper-of-all-things-important, was bustling around the house preparing to leave for work. He hurried over to the dining room table, the well-known family file cabinet, where only he knew the perfect order to the madness of it all, and began ruffling through a giant pile of papers. After a moment, he came back to the kitchen and handed me a sealed envelope.

"Here you go, honey!"

The letter went something like this:

Even though you were born in New York State, you were adopted through Massachusetts courts, so we cannot help you. We have included a brochure for the International Soundex Reunion Registry. Fill out the form to become a member. If either of your birth parents are members, this organization will connect you.

Hmm, interesting, I thought. I filled the form out, stuffed it in an envelope, and handed it to my father, stamped, that very morning, asking him to mail it for me on his way to work. I did so thinking it was just another piece of an extensive puzzle, and it would probably be another five years before I would hear anything more.

Two weeks later, I was sitting in a recliner by the big picture window, waiting for a taxi. I was heading across town to a little sandwich shop where I had been waitressing for the summer. My parents had already left for work; Renée was at basketball practice; I was watching for my ride, when the phone rang.

"Hello?"

"Hello, may I please speak to Danielle Gaudette?"

"Yes, this is Danielle."

The woman's voice on the other end sounded both bright and excited. She introduced herself as Anne Lowry and said, "Danielle, I am calling from the International Soundex Reunion Registry. I am very excited to tell you that I think we have found a match."

A whaaat?!

My stomach dropped to my knees. My heart began to race.

Anne continued, "I need you to gather any and all of the papers you have regarding your biological parents. Any information you have, please get it now. I need to check what you have against the information I have here. I'll hold."

"Okay . . ." My head began to spin.

Without any calculated thoughts, because I was suddenly incapable of making those, my body moved me briskly to the dining room table, the only possible place where such papers might have been.

When I had begun the search for my biological parents eight months prior, my mother had said she would pull whatever she could from the safety deposit box to help me in my quest; however, I had never followed up. I suppose it was because half my brain was still in a pub somewhere outside of the University College Galway.

I rummaged through what looked like the "Danielle pile," and there it was, not far from the top.

"Okay, I have it."

Anne Lowry spoke kindly and carefully, "Please tell me exactly what it says."

Trembling, I began my recitation.

"Description of mother: white, Roman Catholic, Irish descent."

What? I'm Irish? That's so weird. I was just in Ireland. Originally, I had not intended to go to Ireland. I had always planned to go to Spain, but when the time had come, I didn't feel confident enough with the language. I needed to go to an English-speaking country but felt no affinity with the idea of studying in the UK. When I had thought of Ireland, my heart leapt, though I didn't know why. That's how I ended up there.

I read on.

"Five feet five inches tall; weight, 110 pounds; dark brown hair, blue eyes, fair complexion. She is in good health. Experienced an uneventful pregnancy. Mother attended college, majoring in drama. Worked in summer theater and presently is a star in a TV series. Her grandparents (maternal grandparents) are in

43

their fifties, also in good health. Mother is second of six children."

"Yes," Anne said, "Good. And is there information on the father?"

"Description of father: white, Jewish-Russian descent." *Are you serious? I'm Russian?* This took me by surprise even more, seeing that, for no apparent reason, I was completely enthralled with Russian history and literature. During my freshman year at the University of New Hampshire, I had found myself unable to keep up with Intermediate Spanish, yet I still needed to fulfill a language credit. Following a suggestion from my counselor, I had transferred to Russian Culture 101. From the very first class, I was enamored by the stories of the Russian people. After that, taking a Russian language, literature, or culture class every semester became a passion of mine.

I continued.

"Six foot tall, weighing 165 pounds. Has a fair complexion, black eyes, and black hair. He is in good health. No history of serious illness in his background. He is a college graduate. Has a master's degree. He is employed as a theatrical director. Both natural mother and father surrendered child for adoption."

Why I had never known this information about my heritage before that moment, I have no idea. My best guess is that my parents were so completely involved in our family's world, including the stress of my mother's illness, that it hadn't come up. I'd never thought to press the subject. I took the information my parents had given me—that my birth mother had been an actress on a soap opera and was unable to care for me—and didn't question it.

"Well, Danielle," Anne said, "this all matches perfectly with the information we have here in front of us. Yes, we have found your biological mother! We are going to call her now and let her know. I need you to stay by your phone. I'll call you right back."

I began pacing around our apartment in a frenzied loop: living room, kitchen, dining room, living room, kitchen, dining room. My heart was beating so fast there was no way to be comfortably still. Even though it was daytime, I felt it was pitch-black outside. I kept pacing to survive.

The phone rang again. Breathless, I answered.

"Hello, Danielle, it's Anne again. I have very exciting news for you. We are all just so thrilled about it over here in the office. Do you watch *Star Trek*?"

Oh. My. God. No, no, no, no, no . . . please, no. Please don't give me drama right now. I can't take it. No drama. I need this to be normal. Please, God, just give me normal right now.

I grabbed the countertop with my sweaty palms for fear I was going to pass out. In that moment, as my anxiety skyrocketed, I desperately wished for my birth mother to be ordinary. I wished for her to be boring. I wished for her to be a plain woman, living a common life, wearing an unadorned apron in her unembellished kitchen somewhere in suburbia.

I admit, I had a habit of reacting dramatically to every little thing. I was emotionally sensitive, and often my responses to the world around me were blown into greater proportions than necessary. Plus, I was a twenty-one-year-old full of angst about the world and disenchanted with everything in it. Against the system? I guess you could call me that. I only liked trees, boys, and writing poems. Everything else was cause for suspicion. I did my best to respond to Ms. Lowry with the least amount of sarcasm possible.

"No, I don't," I said, trying hard not to reveal that I had never even thought about watching such a show, never imagined that I would, didn't even pay much attention to television in general, and thought, at that time of my life, that it was all quite meaningless.

"Well, your biological mother's name is Kate Mulgrew. She is Captain Kathryn Janeway on *Star Trek: Voyager*. She is sitting in her trailer at Paramount right now, waiting for me to call her back. I want you to hang up your phone and wait for her. She's going to call you right now. Congratulations, Danielle. We are so happy for you!"

Ho-ly shit.

Not holy shit because my biological mother was some famous lady on a television show. Holy shit because the woman who gave birth to me, who brought me into this world, whom I had wondered about in a faraway kind of someday-place in my mind, was about to call me. It was actually happening. Right. Now. There was no more time to think about it. No more time to figure it out. There was not even anyone there to hold my hand. It felt like a ball was hurtling at my face, and I suddenly wasn't sure if I was capable of catching it. The fact that she was currently on a popular television show just made it all the more unbearably dramatic.

The unconscious trauma in my brain that is "being given up for adoption" was now exposed. For Kate Mulgrew, the mother who had to give her baby away, it must have been equally as traumatic. This phone call was yanking the covers off a trauma that had been buried in a deep place inside both of us.

Now, there is a funny thing about trauma—it really messes with the brain. It inserts blankness in places where there should be memories and rewrites the details of stories in twisted and contorted ways. So, according to Kate, it was *I* who called *her* on this day. But in my mind, it was *she* who called *me*. We have discussed this several times since and have concluded that we were both suffering a kind of brain damage at the time. Either of us could be right or wrong, and it absolutely makes not one bit of difference.

What's important is that this was the moment—the moment that came too quickly. I was not prepared. I thought I would be searching for years. But this ultimate moment had been sent down a chute, crashing into me right then and there, and all I could do was let it.

My legs were trembling. My body grew weak. There was a no-place-to-go calm that came over me. I sat down.

The phone rang one more time. I didn't know if I was breathing or not. I pressed the "Talk" button with my cold, wet, index finger, knowing that the person on the other end would be someone whom I had never met, a complete and total stranger, yet somehow, some way, this was the person I was to call my mother.

Three Questions

t's all very sticky and muddy in my mind. It's like a stone path with huge gaps in it. You stand there for a while, trying to figure out how to get to the next stone, then just resolve to drag yourself straight through the mud.

I don't remember that first phone conversation with Kate very well. I don't even remember how it started. It was as if I was straining to hear in a perfectly quiet room. I remember a raspy voice. Was there emotion in it? I remember she was surprised that my voice was not raspy like hers. I remember three questions that came relatively quickly.

Kate: "Are you happy?"

Danielle: "Yes."

Kate: "Are you pretty?"

Danielle: "I don't know. My boyfriend thinks I am."

Kate: "Do you believe in God?"

Danielle: "No."

Well, not in the way you probably mean.

What else did we talk about? I think she went on to tell me that she did believe in God. . . . Something, something . . . something, something.

She was surprised that I was studying in Iowa, as she had grown up in Dubuque. It turned out her mother and brothers lived about twenty minutes away from my campus. So many coincidences.

She told me she wanted to meet me and would that be okay? I agreed. She said she was going to fly to Boston. She would arrive in four days.

Did the conversation last even five minutes? Was it ten? It couldn't have been more than that.

We said our good-byes, and that was it.

Shaking, I picked up the phone again, canceled my taxi, and called work. "I can't come in. I can't explain right now. I'm just not gonna be able to make it today."

The First Meeting

I did not eat a morsel of food, yet I had diarrhea every day for those four days.

On the fourth day, Kate and I were to meet for dinner in the lobby of the Charles Hotel in Harvard Square. My tummy trembled as I looked for parking. *Calm down, Danielle. Please, try to calm down.*

I pushed through the glass doors and entered. There she was—a thin, pretty, well-dressed woman with bobbed, brown hair, standing eagerly, nervously in a lobby full of guests. She must have spotted me first. Although there was nothing about her figure that felt similar to mine, I knew by the way she was approaching me who she was. I knew by the look on her face . . . what was that look? Was it loving? Was it apologetic? Was she about to cry? Was she just as overwhelmed as I? I think so.

We embraced—I think. She was shorter than I. Did we speak? We must have.

We made our way up the short staircase to the restaurant. She kept pouring wine into my glass. Glass after glass of white wine. I was not much of a drinker, but I didn't feel the slightest buzz. I was miles away from my body, reeling. The waiter put a bowl of mixed nuts on the table. I ate a lot of them—even the Brazil nuts. I kept crunching to calm my nerves. I don't even like Brazil nuts.

Or white wine. Did we order food? Chicken, I think. Did I eat it? Barely, I think. What did we talk about? I don't remember much. She asked many questions. I answered them one by one, trying to keep it together.

At some point, we were sitting next to each other, and she said, "Hmm, where did you get those thighs? Those aren't my thighs."

No, I didn't have her thighs, or her body shape at all. She was very small and thin, and I was . . . big. But I had her face, the shape of the jawline, the mouth, the Irish nose and freckles. There it was—my face.

She told me she and my biological father had never married, but she had kept his phone number all these years so she could notify him if she ever found me. She had been looking for me for a long time, she said. She asked me if I wanted to go up to her hotel room to give him a call. I said yes. I could feel the palpitations starting up again.

He was surprised to get the call. His voice was warm and kind, and he was happy to speak with me. At the same time, neither one of us knew quite what to say. His wife got on the phone and eagerly expressed her enthusiasm about our having found each other. They invited me to visit them at their home in Delaware.

"What a great Father's Day gift!" he said, as the call was ending. *Oh, yeah. It's Father's Day . . . I totally forgot to hug my dad when I left the house.* I had forgotten that it was June, or summer for that matter. On the outside, I looked like a regular person; on the inside, I was catatonic.

Next morning, I had planned to introduce Kate to my parents over breakfast. I knew how important it was for all of them to meet, but I was a wreck about it.

When I had originally talked with my mother about arranging for Kate to come to Boston, she was driving us home from my nana's house. She flicked her cigarette ashes out the window, staring dead ahead, not looking at me once. With all the collectedness she could muster, she said, "Okay, honey, whatever you want."

But I'm sure, later that night, in the privacy of their bedroom, when only my father was around, she had probably had a full-blown panic attack.

From early on, my mother had had a recurring nightmare that a rich lady decked in furs showed up at our small apartment, declaring that she was my mother, and took me away. So, even though there were no furs, and I was not going anywhere, this reunion was tearing her up inside. Although she ordinarily shared her emotions with me freely, she would never have shown me her angst in that moment. She supported my decisions with every bit of strength she had, but I could always feel her.

At the most-awkward-breakfast-ever, my father and I excused ourselves to gather food at the buffet, leaving the two mothers alone at the table. While scooping a spoonful of scrambled eggs onto my plate, I glanced over and saw them leaning in, appearing to be in an intense discussion. By the time we got back, they were all smiles and laughter. Kate informed me that they'd just come to an important agreement: Kate agreed with Beverly that Beverly was, in fact, my mother, and that Kate would not try to get in the way of that; and Beverly agreed with Kate that, moving forward, she would allow Kate the chance to build a relationship with me if I wanted it, since I was, after all, her daughter. I just nodded and smiled.

That evening we had a big dinner at Jimmy's Harborside with my parents and almost everyone from my mother's Italian family, the Manzellis. Since my father's soft-spoken, French Canadian parents had died when I was very young, this was my *only* family. They were my people. They marched in one by one: my nana and papa came first, followed by my aunt Gail, my cousin Carly, my uncle Frankie and his wife, Alexa, and, of course, my sister, Renée. They all came to show their support, but they had a secret motive—to let this Kate lady know whose family I was *really* a part of. That was the Manzellis—passionate, overly protective, deeply loving, and, dare I say, dramatic. And there was Kate, foreigner to the tribe.

Since Jimmy's Harborside was a well-known seafood restaurant on Liberty Wharf in downtown Boston, it sometimes attracted celebrities. That night, someone from CBS happened to be sitting at a table near us, recognized Kate Mulgrew, and kept sending her bottles of red wine for the duration of the meal. And we kept drinking them. She started to tell the story of how she gave me up for adoption, and when she did, she began to cry. I was at the other end of the table, so I didn't hear what was going on, but by the time I caught wind of it, my mother *and* my grandmother *and* my aunt were weeping along with her, consoling her.

Worried, I rushed over to make sure they were all right. When I looked around, I realized that even my papa, whom I never saw cry, had tears in his eyes, and my uncle, with his big muscles covered in tattoos, was blowing his nose.

Only my sister was stone-faced. She sat with her head down, fiddling with her phone. Her pain must have been exacerbated by the fact that for her, another adoptee, the door was not open to finding her biological parents. She had an "I don't know what I feel, but I can't really take it" thing going on, so she left early, as she often did, saying she had "something to do."

So, there I was, the only remaining set of dry eyes at the table, comforting each person, one by one, telling them it was okay, that everything was okay.

After dinner, as we drove Kate back to the hotel, I sat next to her in the back seat. She reached for my hand. From the front seat, my mom turned around and held my other hand. Then Kate said, "How does it feel to have two mothers holding your hand?"

How does it feel, you ask? How does it feel?! It feels like all circuits in my brain are shutting down. It feels like everything is coming undone. It feels like something is happening to me, and I don't know what, and I can't really breathe, but I'm trying really hard to keep it together. That's how it feels.

I think I smiled—a nervous, sweaty, lost smile.

Kate got out of the car. We said our good-byes. She was returning to LA the next morning.

As we drove away, I sank down in my seat and leaned my head against the window. The numb, frozen block of ice that my heart had become, from the moment Anne Lowry told me she had found a match, burst open. Unexpectedly, unannounced, it just shattered. I collapsed in a fountain of sobs. My parents tried to comfort me, but there was nothing they could say or do.

I cried for three days.

I have been healing for twenty-three years.

Phoebe Columba Mulgrew

*L*ater that summer, Kate flew me out to LA to visit her world and to meet her sons, my new half brothers. Each time we spoke on the phone to figure out the details of the trip, my head spun.

Kate was unlike anyone I had ever met. Although the Manzelli family was excessively expressive, I was discovering that Kate's persona was much bigger and bolder than any of theirs. Whenever I spoke to her, I felt like I had taken a large bite of a savory, decadent dish—rich with so many flavors that it almost overwhelmed the palate and was more than I could completely digest in one swallow. I was both intimidated and intrigued.

During my flight, I stared out the window, going over the details Kate had begun to share with me from her side of the adoption story. She emphasized how, even though she had been deeply immersed in her work and the blossoming of her career at the time, she had wanted to find a way to keep me. She had asked her mother to help take care of me temporarily, until she could figure things out, but her mother had refused because she was grieving the loss of Kate's younger sister. Tessie had died of a brain tumor at the age of fifteen, only three years before I was born. This loss had devastated her mother and rendered her unable and unwilling to muster the energy and heart it would take to care for a baby.

Kate told me how she was deeply saddened by the decision she was forced to make. Shortly after I was born, she began to fall into despair. She contacted Catholic Charities to try to get some information about me, but, because it was a closed adoption, it was a closed door. They told her, "We can only let you know about her if she dies." Kate could not accept this. She continued to contact Catholic Charities, visiting them in Manhattan from time to time, trying to persuade them to give her something, anything, about me.

Eventually, she hired a private detective, who had found me in Watertown, Massachusetts—a high school senior, looking healthy and well. While Kate was glad to know I was okay, she was also shocked to find out that I was not in New York City. According to her, when she had been preparing to give me up for adoption, Sister Una McCormack, from the Catholic Home Bureau, had allowed her the opportunity to choose what kind of people my adoptive parents would be.

Kate had wanted three things for her baby: she wanted me to remain in New York City, she wanted me to be raised Catholic, and she wanted my parents to be a doctor and an artist. She had chosen a lovely and sophisticated couple who checked all the boxes. Once Kate realized from the private detective that I was not with them and that her request had not been honored, she was furious; she felt she had been betrayed.

This was all very disorienting for me. Sister Una McCormack was the one my parents spoke so highly of, the one who actually *helped* them adopt me. When I told Kate this, she found it even more disturbing.

A few years after the private detective had found me, Kate said that she had unexpectedly run into Sister Una at a fundraiser in Manhattan. She had led the nun over to a quiet corner and demanded, once more, that she give her some kind of information about her daughter. She knew what the Catholic Home Bureau had done; she knew they had broken their agreement; and she insisted they owed her some kind of information. It was then that Sister Una McCormack said something that took Kate by surprise: "Your daughter is looking for you now. As you know, there's little I can do, but I will drop off a brochure for the International Soundex Reunion Registry at your hotel tomorrow morning. Then, I will mail one to your daughter. If you both become members, the organization will connect the two of you. It will be in your hands, both of your hands."

Kate said she had spent nearly my entire life agonizing over her decision to give me up for adoption. Her grief had affected many of her relationships, especially the one with her ex-husband, the father of her boys. She said that my effort to reach out to her, my filling out the Soundex form had, finally, brought her great relief.

Peering down at the dry, brown earth as the plane began its descent, I felt my head full of so much information, so many stories. I had listened to Kate tell them all, and I had wanted to be comforted by them, as I felt that's what they were intended for, but I could hardly take them all in. I was spinning. I'd been spinning from the moment of Anne Lowry's phone call and my time with Kate in Boston. I hadn't stopped spinning. I was on a ride—a wild and crazy carnival ride—and there was no getting off. In a state of complete overwhelm, I landed at LAX on a bright, sunny day.

Just a few hours later, I found myself sitting with Kate on her patio by the pool, sipping an ice-cold glass of San Pellegrino, when Ian, the older of her two sons, came out of the house. I was immediately fascinated by this fifteen-year-old boy. His hair was dark, like mine. I don't think he smiled; I don't think he even grinned. He had a serious look in his eye. He sat down with us, and after a moment of slightly uncomfortable silence, he said, "Well, this is bizarre."

I was impressed by his frankness. Yes, it was bizarre—that's *exactly* what it was. To hear him speak so succinctly of the situation comforted me. I had never done well with small talk, so his candid approach to the moment took the edge off the awkwardness. I was grateful to him for that and felt a sort of kinship.

His brother, Alec, came home a little while later. He was one year younger than Ian and had a different personality entirely. Because of a skateboarding accident, he had a cast that covered his leg all the way up to his hip. Full of a big, jovial kind of energy, he hopped right up to me on his one good foot. He opened his arms wide and, with a smile across his freckly face, called out, "Hey, sis! Gimme a hug!"

At first, it was fun to meet these endearing characters. Actually, that week in California, I met all kinds of characters from Kate's life. I met her ex-husband, several of her dear friends, some coworkers, and a few neighbors. There were even those who came with gifts of flowers and jewelry for me, to let me know just how much I meant to Kate, how important this meeting was, and how grateful they were for me to be there.

Yet, as the week unfolded, I found that a knot had begun to twist in my stomach, and my chest had started to tighten. Ultimately, these people were strangers to me. It unsettled me to realize that I had preexisted for them—especially for Ian and Alec.

At dinner one balmy night, again on the patio by the pool, Kate and her sons talked more about me. Amid glasses of sparkling water and white wine, a fancy array of silverware (Two forks? Did I need two forks?), the live-in housekeeper clearing dirty dinner dishes and dropping off plates of perfectly sliced flan (Flan? What was flan?), my newly found half brothers shared *their* side of the story. Galaxies away from Piermont Street and my simple, suburban, Shake 'n Bake upbringing, I listened as Ian and Alec shared with me that for years they had wondered about their "sister." Ever since they learned about her—me—from their mother when they were eight and nine years old, they thought about their somewhere-out-there sister, talked about her, and hoped for a time when they could finally meet her. They even had a name for her. Kate had given me the name of Phoebe Columba Mulgrew—naming me after Sister Columba, the nun who had comforted her mother when Tessie died.

That night, as the sun set, and they chattered away with excitement, I got a chilling feeling that Phoebe was very much alive in their lives, like a ghost. I felt I had come to LA to fill the shoes of my own ghost.

I was not expecting to suddenly have a new family. I already *had* a family—and I had a strong loyalty to that family. I respected and honored them completely. I mean, those were the people I grew up with, who knew everything about me, who had been there for me my entire life. When Alec asked me, "Do you really think of yourself as my sister? You *are* my sister, right? And I'm your brother?" I saw my own younger sister's face flash in front of my eyes. *No, I don't have any brothers! I only have one sister! Her name is Renée. We played and fought and joked together! We laughed and cried and made memories together!* And when Kate took me around the Voyager set at Paramount, introducing me to her fellow cast members, all of whom understood me to be her daughter, I thought, *No! You are not my mother! I already have a mother. She held me and loved me and took care of me all my life. Isn't she the one who deserves to be called my mother?*

Guilt and resistance began to swell in me. I was building a defensive wall inside my heart. All I could think about was my innocent family on the other side of the country, loving me purely and completely, and here I was, betraying them.

On the other hand, whenever I looked at Ian and Alec, or even at Kate, I felt guilty in another way. I could not wholeheartedly open myself to be the person they wanted me to be.

And who was that person, anyway? Was she Danielle Gaudette? Was she Phoebe Columba Mulgrew? Was she a ghost? Agitation began to cover me like a thin layer of itchy skin. My mind descended into a tangle of chaos.

Losing It

By the time I got back to the University of Iowa, I still couldn't sort out my feelings. One day, my boyfriend, Matt, and I were walking to campus together when I looked down to find that my sandal had unbuckled. I sat on the curb to rebuckle it and realized it was broken. Suddenly, I became frantic and burst into senseless tears. Dumbfounded, Matt asked me why I was crying.

"Because if my sandal is broken, it means my mother is going to die!"

He looked at me in shock, then gently put his hand on my back. "No, it doesn't mean that, Danielle. It doesn't mean anything like that."

Matt knew I was prone to paranoia. He listened to me when I worried obsessively and often talked me down from ledges of nonsensical meaning making: *No*, the little bump on my skin didn't mean I had cancer; *no*, his friend's pet iguana wasn't going to attack me when he was out of his cage; *no*, the tornado hitting hundreds of miles outside of Iowa City didn't mean we all needed to flee for the basement to save our lives. My insecure outbursts were even kind of cute to him when he was able to comfort me, and I was able to shrug the fears off after a moment or two. However, after coming back from LA, my affliction became much darker, more twisted and relentless, and more a cause for his concern.

Another evening, we were on our way to our favorite Indian restaurant. As we were approaching the town center, I stopped in the middle of the sidewalk, and again, this time out of the blue, began to cry. Matt patiently held space for me, waiting for me to pull myself together, but I couldn't. I just cried and cried until he wrapped me in his arms. Collapsing into his safe embrace, I sobbed. "I don't want to be adopted! I just don't want to be! I don't want it!" That was the only clear feeling I could express at that moment. It wasn't that I didn't want my parents to be my parents, or that I didn't want Kate to be my biological mother, I just wished that being adopted was not my predicament in this lifetime.

In opening myself to Kate and her family, I felt I was betraying mine. My mother, father, and sister, who were always there for me and always would be, didn't deserve for me to consider myself a part of anyone else's family. I felt both bad and wrong for doing so. Bad, bad, bad. Wrong, wrong, wrong. These feelings were shrieking in my brain like a murder of crows. That is why, if any other tiny thing went so-called wrong in my life, such as a buckle breaking, it was cause for a breakdown.

Nobody *made* me feel this way. Nobody said a word about me betraying anyone. Nobody said there was any reason to feel guilt, shame, or self-blame. These were feelings I was torturing myself with inside my own mind. On top of them, the thought of pushing Kate away in order to make it all disappear made me feel even more guilty and sorry. It wasn't right, nor was it what I really wanted. I was overwrought with conflict, and if I could have been granted one wish, I would have wished for it all to never have been so in the first place. I would have wished that I was just born of Beverly and Bob Gaudette, and that this adoption business had all been a dream.

It felt as if a bandage had been ripped off a wound I didn't even know I had. The guilt and confusion were the pus of a deep, unseen injury that I didn't yet understand. The wound was oozing and dripping everywhere, beyond my ability to control it.

I desperately wanted to find peace and heal myself from the inside out. I found myself increasingly insecure. Nothing made me happy. I was overwhelmed by life, irritated with therapy, and uninterested in drugs. I couldn't relate to the students at school either. I couldn't connect. What was everybody doing? What was the point of any of it? What did I want? I didn't know.

Not only my world but also the world at large seemed like such a scary and disastrous place. I loved my boyfriend, but as graduation approached, I looked at him and thought, *Is this it? Is this what happens now? I get a job, get a husband, get a kid, get a dog, get a house? Is that supposed to make me happy?* The fact that I knew it would never make me happy made me feel all the more broken. I felt impossibly confused, impossibly dissatisfied, impossibly anxious.

I assessed this mess of feelings and made a decision: if this storm of craziness was in *my* mind, then *I* was the only one who could fix it. No matter what, I was going to find a way to do that—*by myself.*

Red Boats

My neurosis began when I was six years old, shortly after my mother's mental illness was diagnosed. We lived near a graveyard, and every time we drove by, I would think about how, someday, my parents and my grandparents were going to die. This frightened me to the core. Death was just something I could not accept. I couldn't wrap my mind around it. One day, I even begged my nana to promise me she would never die. Just to get me to stop crying, she did.

When I was eight years old, I developed a fear of vomiting. Since I worried so much about everything, at the end of every day, I felt sick to my stomach and thought I was going to throw up. I would then launch into a panic about it, resulting in my mother and me sitting by the toilet bowl, night after night. She'd be right there, holding back my long, black, curly hair, wiping my sweaty forehead with a cool cloth, while I spit out saliva. I can probably count on one hand the number of times I have *actually* thrown up in my life. This neurotic ritual went on for months.

One night, my mother was explaining this predicament to my nana while we were eating pizza at Papa Gino's. My nana turned to me with so much love in her eyes and confidence in her voice and said, "All you need to do, sweetie, is just take small bites of your food and chew really well, and you won't have that problem anymore."

I held on to what she had said as if it was the word of God. I took the tiniest of bites that night and chewed and chewed my pepperoni pizza until it turned to liquid in my mouth.

"You don't have to eat like a bird!" my mother teased me. To which my nana replied, "Leave her alone! Let her do whatever she wants!"

I did. And I never sat in front of the toilet with my mother again.

My anxiety peaked my senior year of high school when I developed a fear of dying and a phobia of all things that could end me: AIDS, cancer, plane crashes—you name it, I was petrified. During my freshman year of college, my fears morphed into global warming, nuclear war, and more cancers that I hadn't even known existed. The more information I took in, the more I twisted it into sheer terror. I lived at a fear level of ten for two solid years. I felt as if there was a dark cloud over my head. I honestly don't remember a single sunny day during that time. I looked around at other people and thought, *Why are you smiling? Don't you know this world is a mess and everyone you love is going to die someday? How could you possibly be happy?* I was going mad. So much so that I walked myself into the campus mental health center, desperate for help.

My assigned therapist's name was Bill, a tall, gray-haired man who may have been in his early sixties. He was so tall he had to duck his head a little when he came out to greet me in the lobby. I followed him into his book-lined office where we sat in oversized leather chairs. He stared at me through his bifocals as I fiddled with the dolphin charm on the end of my necklace. For maybe a solid minute, he watched me nervously shift the trinket side to side while I waited for him to speak—but he was waiting for me.

I ended up telling him all about my life. I told him about my fear, my paranoia, my hypochondria. I told him how I made my nana promise me she would never die. I sobbed as I felt the agony of how those fears had terrorized me my whole life and were only getting worse.

Bill was present, there with me, without adding or subtracting anything, just listening. He mostly let me talk and talk. My eyes darted around his room as I anxiously told him everything about me. I happened to notice several books on Buddhism on one of his shelves. I felt he was a good man. He could have recommended anything to me. My friends who struggled with anxiety and depression were being introduced to Prozac; he never even considered it.

"What do you do when you begin to have fearful thoughts?" he asked.

"I call my mother."

"Okay. From now on, I don't want you to call your mother anymore when you feel this way."

"But why?"

"Because you rely on her to comfort you, but in a short time, the comfort fades, and you are back where you started."

He was right. I hadn't realized it, but he was spot-on. My mother was like a temporary pacifier to all my wild fears.

"Instead, I want you to do this," he said. "I want you to go to a quiet room. Turn off the TV and the radio. Make sure there are no distractions. Just be alone with your fearful thoughts." My heartbeat quickened at the idea of it, but my eyes widened. I was listening with rapt attention.

"In the quiet room, close your eyes and visualize yourself sitting by the bank of a river. Thousands of colorful sailboats are floating freely down that river, passing you by. Those sailboats are like your thoughts, hundreds of them, flowing through your mind all the time.

"Now, let's call your fearful thoughts the red boats. You are focused only on the red boats. You look for the red boats, you grab the red boats out of the water, and you obsess over them. Because of that, you don't see the other colored boats. From now on, I want you to allow all of the colored boats, including the red ones, to pass you by. Let them come and let them go. Quietly observe the colorful sailboats from the bank of the river."

Every word that Bill spoke went deep into my psyche. I held on to them as if they were the cure for my disease. I practiced every day. Every time I had a fearful thought, I did exactly as he instructed. And it worked! The more I did it, the more I felt released from the prison of my fears. Instead of being consumed for weeks at a time by my dreadful thoughts, I could let them come and go, and I could move on with my day. The grip of darkness began to loosen. I remember the day I walked down the street and suddenly realized *It's sunny out! What a beautiful day!* I was alive again.

With diligent practice, I maintained this management over

my fearful thoughts for about four years—until I met Kate. Then, the wire above the lion's den I had been balancing on snapped, and I tumbled into the ferocious pit, only to be devoured by my insanity once more.

Yet, something had been gained. It was my trust in the power of practice, my confidence in the wisdom garnered through self-observation, and my discovery that I was a hardworking student of life who didn't give up easily.

Coming Home

Ki Energy

When I graduated from college and returned home to Boston, Matt came with me to stay at my parents' house temporarily. Four months later, we were set to go to Abiquiu, New Mexico, to intern on an organic farm.

I was more frazzled than ever. After meeting Kate, I worried constantly—a neurotic, irrational type of worry. Whenever people talked to me, including Matt, I listened with about 30 percent of my attention; the other 70 percent of me was perseverating about who knows what. I was constantly unsettled, and this put a strain on my relationships. I felt as if the little hairs around my forehead were burned and frayed wires sticking out in all directions.

"Mom, I need yoga."

"Well, honey, I saw a place just down the street on my way home from Target the other day. There's a big yellow sign outside that says 'Yoga, Tai Chi, Meditation.'"

"Sounds perfect."

It was my mother, my angel, who first spotted the Body & Brain Center. I don't know if I would have ever seen it myself. It was in such a remote spot, behind a gas station, above a dry cleaner, in a small parking lot. Fortunately, that big yellow sign was facing the street where my mother often idled, waiting at the red light, nursing her favorite Dunkin' Donuts iced coffee. It must have been divine providence.

What I first fell in love with during my initial week of classes at the center were the two instructors. I was intrigued by them. They seemed heavenly. They were the most authentic people I had ever met. I felt more connected with them than I had with anyone I had encountered in school. They were soft and warm-hearted, with a bright aliveness in their eyes. They had an aura of peace and light, and I found myself wanting to be around them for as long as I could.

This was even more striking because, being from Korea, neither one of them was proficient at speaking English. The head trainer, Chun Shim, was better at it than her assistant, Lee. Chun Shim had a Yoda-like magic about her. I always felt deeply honored to receive the wisdom she delivered during our teatime sessions after class. We all sat in half-lotus on the floor, gathered around an Asian-style tea table in a ceremonial sort of way, sipping on freshly brewed herbal tea and sharing our class experience.

After about two weeks of practice, I started noticing that there was something very different about this yoga from the Kripalu yoga I had taken when I was in Iowa City. Of course, I had loved those yoga classes too. I had always left feeling refreshed, calmer, and happier, but, by the time I had walked over the bridge, crossed campus, passed through downtown, and arrived at my apartment, I would be in a bad mood all over again.

Body & Brain was different.

The most notable result came from the ki-energy meditation that we did in every class. In sitting posture, we would raise our hands to face each other, move them closer and farther apart without touching, and try to feel the sensation between our palms. From the beginning, I was mesmerized by the magnetic force between my hands. This exercise was called *ji-gam*, which simply meant to stop your thoughts and emotions. While I was feeling that palpable push-and-pull sensation, my mind would grow quiet, deeply still. When the meditation was over, I would feel clear and bright. I began to notice this feeling staying with me for days at a time. The more I went to class, the more I was able to sustain it, until I woke up one day, thinking, *I'm not mad at the world today. Wow, it's even more powerful than the red boats! Something's changing!*

The more positive I felt, the more I wanted to spend time at the center. I began to stay after class to drink another cup of healing tea, to read through a book, or to practice my ji-gam meditation just a little while longer.

I felt most alive when I was at the center—the hidden gem that was tucked behind a gas station, above a dry cleaner. The floor vibrated from the machines below, and from time to time, there might be pigeons roosting in the rafters, but for me, it was a place of magic and wonder, a place of love and authenticity where I felt rescued from the insanity of the world.

Enjoying a breath of sweet freedom from my negativity, I began to attend classes every day. In the third week, Chun Shim approached me after teatime. She sat me down, looked into my eyes, and asked me a life-changing question: "Do you want to find your True Self?"

I felt as if she had seen into the bottom of my heart. Something leapt inside of me. It was as if I had been waiting for someone to ask me this question for my entire life.

"Yes! Yes, that's what I want more than anything! I want to know the truth of me that's underneath all the noise and chaos. Can you really help me find it?"

Chun Shim smiled gently and nodded with that Yoda-like sparkle in her eyes, as if to say, "Yes, young Padawan. Yes, I can."

My Soul

Awakening and transformative is how I would describe the Finding True Self workshop, but those are just words and do not scratch the surface of what I felt or how the experience impacted me.

I brought to that workshop a sincere desire to find some sort of peace inside. I was tired and lost, and tired of being lost. I was only twenty-two years old, but I felt there was nothing this world had to offer that could bring me any fulfillment, unless I found peace and truth inside myself first. I was desperate to find it. That pure wish was my fuel.

At the workshop, I dug into my heart with sweat and tears. I went down deep, through layers of judgment and emotion, memories and wounds. In the most challenging of moments, I pushed forward, believing there must be something beyond this suffering. There just had to be.

After a very intense session, an assistant was leading us through a breathing meditation. As I rested on the floor, she guided us to relax each part of the body. I quieted my mind and sank into feeling the top of my head, my eyes, my face muscles, my jaw, my neck, my shoulders. Suddenly, there was an unexpected and very loud *crack* in the center of my chest. It felt like the wall of a dam had broken open, and a warm, soft river of love was flowing through my heart. For the first time ever, I felt completely silent; I felt the peace I had been longing for; I felt bliss.

It was an unforgettable feeling that happened in a moment. It was not something I came to understand with my thoughts. It was not something I had learned from someone else. It was something I *felt* inside of me.

I had met with my soul.

I had found the light inside. I had discovered the purest, deepest, truest me that was buried beneath a lifetime of fear and insecurity, anger, sadness, and confusion—the most beautiful me. I wished I could hold that precious me tenderly in my hands, admire the magnificence of its soft light that seemed to emanate all the love and peace in creation. This light felt like my most beloved friend and guide. Our long-awaited meeting was more, much more, than I could have ever dreamed.

When I returned to my parents' house, my mother swung open the door and said, "You're back!" Then she paused as she looked at me and said, "And you look so . . . *happy!*"

For weeks, I was in a magical state. I would be walking home and find tears of gratitude flowing down my cheeks—gratitude for the amazing force of life that I felt inside.

One evening, as I was sitting on my front steps, watching the sunset, I realized, *I'm falling in love with myself.*

I had found my True Self, my home, and it had been right there within me all along.

Breaking Free

Four months sped by. Matt and I had purchased a tent, gear, and all that we needed for our first-ever farming adventure. In college, I had decided I wanted to learn how to farm organically so, when I graduated, I could travel around the world with WWOOF (Worldwide Opportunities on Organic Farms) until I found my purpose. Matt was mostly just following me. I had told him, "This is what I'm going to do when I graduate. You can come if you want. Or not. It's your choice." He chose to come. He was a gentle, loving, supportive guy, but I had always felt a missing piece in me. I was yearning for something and searching for what that was. I thought traveling and digging my fingers into the earth would show it to me, and nobody was going to stop me from that quest.

One week before leaving, something unexpected happened. I had been connecting daily to my soul and spending a lot of time practicing at the center, when another Finding True Self workshop appeared on the schedule. This time, I pleaded with Chun Shim to allow me to participate as staff. I felt it would be my great honor to assist others along their sacred journey inward, a journey that had been so transformative for me. It was agreed that I would be allowed to be part of the "outside staff."

For two days, my friend Genia, the other outside staff member, and I ran around doing small jobs—prepping lunch and tea, buying extra pens and paper, setting out fruit and nuts for breaks. When we were not busy running errands, we were instructed to sit quietly and meditate, sending energy into the classroom for the participants to have a healing experience. When the most intense part of the workshop arrived, we were finally given the chance to enter and support the process from the back of the room.

As I stood there watching the trainees that day, a mystical feeling came over me. I felt myself inside a huge field of cosmic energy, and in that space, it was as if I had new eyes—eyes of clarity. I looked around the room and saw a lot of people working hard to overcome their egos. It suddenly became apparent to me that each one of them was inside their own bubble of self-imposed hell. *I* wasn't in that hell at that moment, but they were. I realized that each of us creates our own inner hell, that *I'd* been creating my own inner hell all along, and it seemed so very sad to me.

Compassion welled up inside my heart. I felt we had all become lost in our own version of misery, accepting it as truth, but it wasn't the actual truth, it was just our illusion. It was up to each one of us to use our will to get ourselves out of it, to break ourselves free.

As I was awakening to this truth, a clear voice spoke to me. It was my own inner voice, giving me a message that vibrated through my brain and heart: "I have come to the earth to help souls wake up."

I felt this voice so deep inside I knew for certain it was true. I knew for certain I had found my one, clear purpose.

You'd think I would have leapt out of bed the next morning full of joy and light. But no. I woke up with a deep, heavy sadness. I dragged myself around not knowing where this depression was coming from. It was not until I took myself to the center later that day for my training that I burst into tears. I told Lee, "I don't want to leave Boston now!"

To which he replied, "What *do* you want?"

I ended up crying the entire week. I didn't know what I wanted, and I didn't know what to do. I felt responsible to keep my commitment to the farmer who was waiting for us, and I didn't want to break that promise. I was nervous about disappointing Matt and my parents if I changed my plan. I wanted to be a reliable girlfriend and daughter who kept her word. But I really didn't want to leave. My heart felt so heavy and sad at the thought of going.

Two days before our scheduled departure, I finally got what I needed to help me make my decision. I was lying on my bed with my hands on my abdomen, following my breath in and out, trying to calm my mind, when a small voice came forward from my soul. It spoke simply and innocently: "You were looking for me. You found me. So why are we leaving now?"

Everything became clear. I had been wanting to go on my farming adventure to find myself, but I had found what I was looking for before I had even left. There was no longer a need for that journey. Another journey had already begun, and it was right there inside of me. I needed to stay in the place where I could go deeper into what I had discovered and move toward actualizing my purpose. I needed to make this choice for the growth of my soul.

That night I sat down with Matt and told him of my change in plans. I explained that, although it was not an easy decision, I knew with everything inside of me that I needed to stay and do this. I told him, "You can stay here with me if you want. Or you can go. It's your choice."

This time, Matt decided to go.

His best friend took my place so the farmer could have his two interns, as he'd expected. It all worked out as well as it could. As for our relationship, Matt and I hung on for a couple more years, but we had been fractured by that choice. The moment we said good-bye at the train station, our relationship was never quite the same.

I was making a new choice—a choice to dive, headfirst, into my internal growth and development. The more I grew, the more I felt distant from Matt. I felt unsatisfied. There was a depth missing between us that I was hungering for, and I wanted freedom to pursue my desire to reach that depth that was burning within me.

What I truly wanted in that moment was to dedicate my entire self to my inner work and to the path that lay before me—a path of helping other souls wake up. I knew it with every cell in my body. I had found my life's purpose, and there was only one way forward: to devote myself to a life of choosing for my soul.

I'm Sorry

*A*fter Matt left, I was looking forward to having time alone to work on myself. A fellow member from the center was searching for someone to house-sit her condo for six months while she was in Africa. I jumped at the opportunity.

Every morning, I woke up at 4:00 a.m. to do my training. I would go down to the basement for my 103 bows (prostrations), then stand with slightly bent knees, tailbone tucked, and tap my lower abdomen rhythmically with my fists for forty minutes. Every evening, I would stay up late, meditating, opening my meridian channels, and cleaning out negative memories through various tapping and breathing exercises.

One night, I was working on a particular meditation where I would recall a negative emotional memory, feel it, see it, then smile at it as I exhaled. This released deep tension from my brain and allowed me to let go of the intense emotion tied to the memory. I was recalling my mother's illness, her breakdowns, and how they caused turmoil in our life on Piermont Street—all experiences that evoked sadness in me. As I exhaled with a smile, the sadness began to loosen and transform into an overwhelming feeling of responsibility, then transform once more into a feeling of rage. The memories shifted into those of my angry teenage years when I wanted to escape, when I was mad at everyone around me, when I yelled and swore and became aggressive.

Suddenly, I was drenched in a feeling of deep remorse that caught me by surprise. Although I continued to smile as I breathed out, I began to cry. Tears just kept coming like a geyser erupting. Even though my heart ached, it felt good to cry. It felt right—I knew what I needed to do.

I picked up the phone and dialed.

"Hello?" said the voice on the other end. It was my sister. She was not much of a phone picker-upper, and it was late, so I felt fortunate she had answered.

"Hi, Née."

"Belly? Are you okay? Are you . . . crying?" She still used my childhood nickname. Somewhere along the line, Danielle became Danielly-Belly, which became Belly Button. To this day, several of my family members still call me plain old Bell or Belly.

"Née, I'm just calling because I wanted to tell you I'm sorry. I'm really sorry. I know I hurt you a lot when we were little, and I'm so, so sorry about it. I really hope you will forgive me."

There was a long pause. I just sniffled and whimpered, waiting for Renée's response. Finally, she spoke, her voice quivering. "Don't ever say that to me again," she said. I knew that was her way of telling me that she forgave me. We both cried together for a bit.

"I love you so much, Née."

"I love you too, Belly Button. Don't cry. It's okay."

And that was it. Ever since that conversation, we have grown closer with each passing year. She told me one Christmas, over an espresso martini, that my phone call to her that night was a game changer. It absolved some damage that had been done, and her heart had opened to me in a new way. It gave me a chance to try again to be the big sister I had always wanted to be. I'm so grateful for the healing power of "I'm sorry."

Healing Water

The more I transformed the hurt in my heart, the more I was eager to help others do the same. I wanted to become an expression of the light I had discovered inside. After a year of diligent training in Boston, I returned once more to the retreat center in Sedona, the place where I had experienced the Healing Tree within me, to take the initial course to become a trainer myself.

One of the most powerful sessions of the course was the making of "healing water." The purpose of the exercise was to make healing water through a practice of loving concentration. The trainer placed a glass of water in front of each student. We were told to hold it with both hands, at eye level, for forty-five minutes, while imbuing the water with our sincere intention.

"Think about the person you would like to make this healing water for," the trainer said.

I didn't have to think. I knew who it was. My mother.

As I held up the water, I wept, looking back at how this single-most wish had defined my life, how long I had desperately yearned for my mother to heal. That wish was ingrained in my brain, my heart, my every waking moment. It was the air I breathed. It was a constant ache, a source of great sorrow.

As I cried, a new awareness flickered in my mind. It was

the realization that all the effort I had poured into taking care of my mother's mental and emotional well-being had cultivated something inside of me. Starting from the time I was six years old, every tear I wiped, every comforting word I shared to calm her anxiety, and every song I sang to make her smile had developed in me a compassionate heart. I had learned, as a small child, how to nurture. Although I hadn't recognized it, my mother's sickness had already awakened a healer's mind within me.

As I stared at the glass of water, it was as if my whole life reorganized itself. I saw that I had created a fixed belief, a negative pattern in my brain that went like this: my mother was mentally ill → it was so painful for me → that's why I am depressed → life is hard.

The depth of my prayer in that moment, the recognition of the deep longing for her healing that I had endured, penetrated that negative pattern, and the purity of my soul now showed me another perspective. My brain circuits rerouted, giving birth to a new, healthier belief: my mother was mentally ill → it was so painful for me → I did my best to help her → through helping her, I cultivated a healer's mind within me → it was her suffering that led me to my soul's path in this lifetime → I am so grateful for the perfection of my journey.

My bitter tears turned sweet as my awakening came clear: I had been training for this very moment since I was six years old! Everything had happened as it was intended. With one small shift of perspective, my heart opened, and I was humbled by the beauty of it all. I had set out to pour my love for my mother into that water, but what I got in return was an amazing gift of healing that purified my own mind and transformed my perspective on my life.

When the training was over, we were instructed to taste the water that had been imbued with our loving intention. The soft, light liquid soothed my body and satiated my spirit. Each sip felt like a sacred tribute to my mother, my great trainer.

My Primal Wound

*n*ot long after my experience with the healing water, my mentor told me I had cleaned up my childhood hurts. "All you have to do now," she said with an encouraging smile, "is heal the pain that remains from your birth parents."

This was not the news I wanted to hear.

How could I possibly heal the part of my brain that felt so very numbed, blocked, closed off, *blind* to me? I couldn't grasp that part of myself. Or maybe I didn't want to. Maybe I resisted the very thought of it. What was I even reaching for anyway?

It was not until many years later that I realized what I needed to heal: my primal wound—the psychological, energetic injury that happened when I was separated at birth from my biological mother. Understanding this wound, let alone healing it, was like unraveling the great mysterious blind spot in my psyche. In some ways, I'm still disentangling that mystery today.

Meeting Kate slowly brought into view a hurt that had been hidden from my awareness, buried deep in my subconscious. I didn't feel "ready" to face those feelings, but it was time.

What did I find when I delved into the numb and confused parts of my brain? For starters, crippling insecurity, massive trust issues, and deep, pervasive fear. I had to undergo a long process of training myself in how to *lean into* those feelings. I knew that if I didn't allow myself to feel them, I would never be able to purify them. I knew they would control me for the rest of my life and suffocate my soul.

In the early days of the process, I could not find a way to express what I was going through to anyone, especially to Kate. Back then, we were meeting several times a year—either she would come to visit me, or I would go to visit her. I enjoyed dining and drinking wine with her, having a cup of hot tea with her, or lying on a cushy hotel bed, watching movies with her. She was fun and funny, and I wanted to be close to her. At the same time, I wanted to protect myself from her. Something inside me always felt a bit strained, a bit stressed, a bit guarded in her presence.

One night, at a diner in Manhattan, I attempted to communicate with Kate about my deeper struggles, but I was having a hard time. I felt so stuck and mad and sad and needy and nervous and judgmental of my every thought. This mishmash of feelings had tangled into one giant seething ball in the center of my chest.

I told her, "There's a volcano at the bottom of my heart. It's hard to express myself because of it."

"Fuck the volcano!" she said. "Just tell me what you're trying to say!"

I laughed, but all I could do was look down at my french fries and squirm.

I didn't have the clarity at that time to describe what I was trying to say. Was that volcano anger? Rage? Resentment? There's no reason why I shouldn't have felt those feelings. Even Kate, herself, had said to me once, "You must be *so* angry with me."

If I was angry with her, I couldn't access it. Usually, I suppressed any anger I felt because I wanted to be a good person, a nice person. With her, it wasn't even clear to me what I needed to be angry about. It wasn't like I could say, "Hey, Kate! Remember that time you gave me up for adoption? I'm really angry about that." It wasn't possible. There was no straight line to that feeling, no active memory. I didn't *feel* anything about it. That part of me was numb. Blank.

Rather than feeling angry about an event I had no conscious recollection of, I just lived with an injured sense of self. I was overwrought with insecurities and a debilitating lack of confidence. I felt weak, exhausted, as if I had no floor to stand on, no wall to lean on. Still, I had to stand up, I had to walk, I had to *live*.

To survive, I tried to control everything. What else are worry and neurosis if not desires to control the uncontrollable? Attempting to manage the unpredictable nature of being human at every waking moment made me exceedingly tense. I was perpetually clenched like a fist, inside and out.

Then there was guilt. It was the thin transparent veil covering everything else. Why should I be guilty? What had I done? I didn't know. But I *always* felt like I was wrong or bad in some way. I blamed myself for everything. I blamed myself when loved ones didn't return my calls, when boyfriends wanted to break up with me, whenever I got sick, whenever I failed at anything I was working on. In my mind, those common occurrences happened to me because I was somehow not good enough, not right enough for this world.

As I sat across the table from Kate that night, I became

aware that I couldn't hear what she was trying to tell me. Her lips were moving, and she was trying to talk her way through this awkward moment for both our sakes, but there was a crazed girl in my head screaming, "You'd better love me! I need you to love me!" The volcano within had begun to spew.

It surprised me at first—to hear this voice inside of me so clearly—but then I realized she had always been there. She felt . . . familiar. Who was this screaming girl, exactly? She was my anger if it could shout; she was my guilt if it could wail; she was my fear if it could cry out; she was the entity of the wound living inside of me, and I had finally begun to hear her.

I remember nothing more from that night at the diner. I couldn't "just tell" Kate what I was trying to say; I had choked on my primal wound.

Forgiveness

*E*very time I saw Kate after that night, I became more aware of the little girl's voice shrieking inside of me. The wound that was buried, that I couldn't access, always showed up, uninvited, whenever Kate and I interacted. The things Kate said or did not say, the things she did or did not do—it all sent me tumbling down into the dark hole in my sidewalk. I had to climb myself out of that impossibly confusing hole, again and again and again.

After seventeen years of occasional weekend meetings with Kate, seventeen years of climbing out of that hole, seventeen years of processing that screaming voice, Kate invited me to join her in Seattle on her book tour for *Born with Teeth*. We were on stage during a Q&A session when a woman from the audience asked me, "Do you feel that you have forgiven Kate? And if yes, how were you able to do that?"

"Yes, of course," I replied, "I couldn't *not* forgive her."

But in the days that followed, I ruminated over that question. Had I answered honestly? After all, what is this thing called forgiveness? Saying "I'm sorry" was one thing—it was easy to admit the things I felt regretful about. However, saying "I forgive you" was another thing entirely, because it meant recognizing that the other had wronged me in some way.

In the beginning, I didn't have a conscious feeling that I needed to forgive Kate. To forgive her would have meant that I felt she had done something to hurt me, but I didn't consciously feel hurt for being given up for adoption. I adore my parents. It was my great blessing to have them as my mother and father. In fact, I often feel it was a choice my soul made, and it wasn't going to be any other way. My soul was determined to be born onto this earth by Kate Mulgrew, and it was determined to be raised by Beverly and Bob Gaudette. I am confident this was no coincidence.

When I reunited with my biological mother, she so much wanted to be a part of my life that I felt there was no other thing for me to do but open my heart to her—to the best of my ability. From that perspective, it is true, I couldn't *not* forgive her.

As time passed, however, and I began to know Kate, I became overly sensitive and easily hurt in my relationship with her. For a long time, she was the person who could really brighten or break my heart. Present-day hurts began to accrue, and forgiveness needed to occur.

It became increasingly obvious to me that these small hurts were manifestations of a much deeper and larger issue inside me. If she said something a certain way, I felt *extremely* devalued, unsupported, and unloved. If she didn't do something I had wanted or hoped for, I felt *incredibly* rejected, small, and disrespected.

Conversely, if Kate showed me love, gave me recognition, or helped me in any way, I felt *completely* empowered, confident, and upheld. I felt safe.

The size and weight of these contrasting feelings didn't match up with what was happening on the surface. There was a dramatic seesaw in my heart, and I was desperate to heal the imbalance.

The truth was, I wanted to forgive Kate, but I didn't know how.

Karma

$\mathcal{C}$ aught in an endless loop of struggle, I prayed for clarity. I started to wonder if my agony about Kate was related to something beyond this lifetime, if perhaps I was processing some kind of deep karma between us.

Serendipitously, while working in Santa Fe, networking for Body & Brain, I happened to meet a woman who channeled the Akashic Lords (nonphysical Light Beings who govern the Akashic Records, the archives of every thought, experience, and emotion for all souls—past and present). Although the woman made her living as a financial adviser, she happened to have a unique gift for accessing information regarding the path that souls have walked. I had never heard of such a thing, nor was I usually into psychic readings, but I do believe in signs. I got the feeling I needed to ask this medium for help.

She never even took any money. She asked me to email her an important question I wanted to ask the Lords. When she received an answer from them, she would reply.

So I emailed her:

This is regarding my biological mother who gave me up for adoption at birth. Can you tell me anything important about our karma, past lives, or what I need to do or focus on now for me to be healthier, stronger, more peaceful in moving forward in my life? I really want to overcome the heavy karma and trauma that I feel. Any important information about us will be helpful. Thank you.

A couple of months later, she replied.

The Lords' Answer:

Our Dearest Heart,

Let us tell you a story, Dear Child, if you might permit us. Once upon a "past" era, in the space of Earth's time frame that you cannot remember, there were two entities that played the roles of sisters. During this time and space, humans were much less enlightened than they are now, and thus the lives of these two sisters were quite frightful and fraught with peril. Life was hard and disease was abundant and rampant on this planet.

These two sisters had both parents and their other sibling perish from whooping cough and existed in a one-room shack with little in the way of nourishment and heat to keep their vessels warm. They made do with the kindness and charity of neighbors who made them clothes and brought them whatever small amounts of extra food when they could. The sisters, as you can imagine under these circumstances, became quite close, and their "world" became the two of them helping each other to survive. It was quite an unfortunate occurrence, you see.

As you might have guessed, you were the older sister, and your now biological mother played the younger sister. She depended on you for her very existence, and you worked hard at protecting her welfare and very life. You were fiercely protective of her and gave her the food you had first, making sure she was nourished before you. What a model of selflessness you played in that life, Sweet One! One day, when you were twenty and three, a trader passed through and came upon your doorstep. He saw the small garden that you had cultivated out of necessity in your yard and knocked on your door. You see, he was traveling to his next destination to deliver his wares and was hungry, as there had been no resting place for the last thirty miles. As your sister hid behind your skirts, you spoke to this man and let him in for a meal. Upon talking over the food, you and he realized and recognized a Love under the surface. He stayed on for a few weeks and helped you with the chores, cutting wood for warmth for your fire, fixing and making the house stronger, and teaching you with stories at night about the world and the sights he had seen in his travels.

Alas, the time came for him to complete his journey, to sell his wares, and get compensation. His journey would take another two weeks. By this time, he had completely fallen in Love with you and could not bear to be parted from you. He asked you to go with him but thought the trip would be too dangerous and hard for a girl the age of your younger sister. Your heart was torn—do you go with him, or stay with your sister? Oh, what to do? Night after night, day after day, you agonized over this dilemma. Finally, the Heart won out, and you decided to accompany him on his travels for a few weeks. You put your sister into the care of your neighbor and assured her you would be back shortly with coins and food.

Her heart was broken as you rode away with him. She suffered greatly in your absence and became convinced you had abandoned her for good. Tears became her best friend and despair clouded her eyes to the sights of the world. She was a broken child at the age of ten and six.

Four weeks in Earth time later, you and your beau returned. You had fewer coins than planned but still enough food to last through the winter for all of you. You reunited with your sister. However, the damage had been done, and she continued to look out at the world through clouded eyes filled with hurt and a feeling of abandonment. As you saw what she had turned into, you became bent with guilt, and ultimately walked hunched over with a hump on your back, literally carrying around your huge guilt on your shoulders.

Your sister lived with you and your husband for the remaining years of your lives. You continued to always care for her very well-being and welfare in that life, even though you enjoyed a rich relationship with the man. Your guilt would not allow you to suggest her living on her own, would not allow you to let her go apart from you again. She, on the other hand, never got over the abandonment, in her eyes, and therefore always felt unsafe without you by her side. We disclose this past life to you to explain the reasons you planned your birth the way you did in this life. Do you see? Your Souls are always planning the optimum Path for life lessons, and now the lessons are reversed so that both you and your mother can experience the feelings each other went through in the prior life. You will both now know how it felt to experience being abandoned, having guilt, and feeling unwanted. There are no mistakes, Our Dear. All is perfectly planned. There is Divine Order in all. Know this. Now it is time for you to face these feelings and accept them with Love. It is part of your Soul's advancement to do so. We would like to remind you that this was all planned out with the utmost thought and Love. These "feelings" that so pervade your journey this time around are, in reality, nothing more than life lessons that can be learned and released. Do you understand?

Dearest One, we say to you, let these feelings come up in front of you without fear. Acknowledge them, thank them for their lesson, then release them and be free. Child, let go of their hold on you, for that is all just illusion. You have all you need already inside of you, no? Your biological mother cannot hurt you any longer, for her actions were cloaked in Divine Love and her true entity loves you without recourse. What better gift could she have given you than this experience, for now you truly understand those "feelings" that your "sister" had of being unwanted and abandoned; and now she truly understands your prior feelings of overwhelming guilt, no? It has come full circle, as karma always does, you see. Rejoice in the wisdom and planning of these lessons for you both. It is the Divine Plan at work.

Walk in Light and Love, Sweet One. And so it is.

I Forgive Myself

The reading from the Akashic Lords made so much sense to me. Oddly, I did feel a bit like an older sister to Kate. She was much more light-spirited and easygoing than I was. I tended to get weighed down because I took things too seriously and felt burdened by excessive feelings of responsibility for myself and the world. She often asked me for advice on things as well. "I value your wisdom," she would say.

I read the message from the Akashic Lords over and over again. It comforted me deeply. Of course, it was just another story, another piece of information, and it was mine to take or leave. I decided to take it, regardless of whether that story was literal or not. I wanted to use what I felt it had to teach me to help myself in my healing process.

The reading shed light on the place where my enormous guilt was coming from. Perhaps this was why I had always felt bad or wrong in some way. I came to feel that part of the reason why I had come to the earth this time around was to purify any last remaining bits of that previous-life guilt. This story suggested a reason why I seemed to be sorry all the time—deeply and impossibly sorry. My guilt had shrunken my sense of self to the size of a pea, which is why I had become dedicated to recovering my True Self.

The Akashic Lords also eliminated any potential notion that I was a victim of anything in this life. I was able to see that everything was happening perfectly, as it was meant to happen—in fact, as I had *wanted* it to happen. That simple story helped me rewrite my poor-me story.

I came to understand that it wasn't my place to "forgive" others, because everything has its reason. I cannot always know that reason. I cannot know what kind of journey another soul is on, what kind of road that soul has walked or why. All I can do is focus on my own path.

Ultimately, what I realized was that *I* was the one who needed forgiveness. For how unkind I had been to myself in my own head for all of my life, I needed to forgive myself. For not loving myself enough, for not feeling wanted, for torturing myself with those feelings, I needed to forgive myself. For feeling that I deserved the suffering, the rejection, the self-blame, I needed to forgive myself. It was my own perception that had hurt me.

I never gave myself what I wanted others to give me. I rejected myself, and every time I did, I was abandoning my own soul. I needed to forgive myself for all of that.

As the forgiveness process unfolded, I began to feel that beneath it all, my soul was still shining, untarnished. It was always there, ready to love me, ready to embrace me, ready to forgive me unconditionally, at any moment. There was nothing I could have ever done to change that.

The more I forgave myself, the more my heart opened to Kate. I began to look at her with new eyes. She, too, was a soul on a journey. This was not the first time our paths had crossed, but this was an important time. If that past life was true, then everything was completely fair. I understood it all. Maybe this was karma, evening itself out. Maybe this is what healing was all about. Compassion grew, until one day, I discovered that, at the bottom of my heart, there was, and always had been, pure love for her. All my suffering had come out of that one deep desire: I wanted to love my biological mother.

This pure love in my heart that I feel for her is my own love, always there, and I can give it anytime I choose. No one can take it away from me. If I suppress my love for fear of being hurt, that is my choice, that is my loss, and that is my self-inflicted misery. To begin to forgive myself is to liberate my love from the self-imposed prison of my pain.

There is no quick fix for dissolving karma, but forgiving myself, and loving with a love that is beyond conditions are important ingredients.

A Prayer of Forgiveness
—Unknown

If I have harmed anyone in any way, either knowingly or unknowingly, through my own confusions, I ask their forgiveness.

If anyone has harmed me in any way, either knowingly or unknowingly, through their own confusions, I forgive them.

And if there is a situation that I am not yet ready to forgive, I forgive myself for that.

For all the ways that I harm myself, negate, doubt, belittle myself, judge, or be unkind to myself through my own confusions, I forgive myself.

Mercy

Despite our busy lives, Kate and I have made genuine efforts to get together over the years. Due to the pandemic, 2020 was the first year I did not see her in a long while.

I would often visit her in Manhattan. I loved barreling down the Henry Hudson Parkway during my forty-five-minute taxi ride from JFK to Kate's apartment. The thrill of holding on for dear life while the cabby chatted away in his thick New York accent, of watching the bridges, the river, the medley of people going about their days amid tightly packed buildings—all let me feel the strong pulse of human life. Sometimes, I would even get an eerie feeling, as if I had once lived in this city myself! Even though I had left New York ten days after I was born, I had always felt an odd familiarity whenever I returned. When Kate took me to see *Phantom of the Opera*, to shop at Eileen Fisher, or to dine at Carmine's, our jumping in and out of taxis and bustling through the city streets made that familiar feeling come alive.

If I wasn't visiting Kate, she would come see me wherever I was working. We munched on burgers at the Cherry Cricket in Denver, were entranced by the mountain view at the opera house in Santa Fe, and sipped margaritas as we rode the Ferris wheel overlooking Seattle's city lights. We had many walks, many laughs, and many cozy chats in hotel rooms sprinkled across America.

For several years, I spent Thanksgiving with Kate and my half brothers in California. Ian would come from Santa Barbara, Alec from LA, and Kate would fly in from New York, taking a break from her *Orange Is the New Black* filming.

She would rent a beautiful home for us all, stock the kitchen with more food than we could eat, and prepare us an amazing holiday meal.

Always, we were engaged in conversation. One year we sat around a gaslit fire pit, under the stars, reciting our favorite poetry. Another year, we took turns sharing odd dreams that we had had and offering possible interpretations for them. But the time that most stands out in my mind was when we went around the table, sharing what we were grateful for about one another.

That year, Kate's sharing took me aback.

She expressed her gratitude to Ian for the wisdom he embodied, to Alec for the joy he brought to her life, and when she came to me, she spoke of mercy. She said she had learned from me about mercy, and for that she was grateful.

The word struck me. *Mercy.* It echoed in my mind. It seemed like such a strong and powerful word, and not one I was expecting her to use when referencing me. It made me think of church. Wasn't it something you asked the Lord for? Was I really worthy and deserving of such a word?

I'm sure she explained further, but I had not been comfortable enough to expose the fact that I wasn't digesting what she was saying. When I went back to my room that evening, I was still struggling to wrap my mind around what she might have meant. I decided to Google the word: "Mercy: compassion or forgiveness shown toward someone whom it is within one's power to punish or harm." (Oxford Languages)

That was it. *Within one's power to punish or harm.* Punish or harm. Punish or harm. Did Kate really feel that it was within my power to punish or harm her all these years? Was she living with that feeling deep inside?

That night, I realized something I had not previously been aware of: Kate's part, Kate's *heart*, in all of this. Kate's guilt. Kate's shame.

All this time, I had been busy feeling my own pain and examining our relationship from my own point of view, from the depth of my own ability to observe myself. It had been all about *me*. It was about *my* suffering, *my* struggle. Although I had certainly developed compassion in the face of being adopted, it was mostly through opening compassion toward myself, feeling a sense of forgiveness, and a letting go. But I had not yet taken the time to stand squarely in Kate's shoes and see through Kate's eyes. I hadn't had the maturity, the power, the strength of heart, nor the wisdom to do so.

After that visit to California, I allowed myself to imagine what Kate's pain might have felt like. I could sustain it only for brief moments at a time, but when I did, I felt a different kind of weight—not my own weight, but hers—the weight that she must have carried for my entire life. I felt sorry, truly sorry, that I had been unable to recognize it. I had been so consumed with myself, absorbed by my own suffering. Even though I had heard Kate recount her heartache time and again, my ears had been closed, and my heart had been numb to it.

It was maybe a year or two later, after *Born with Teeth* had been published and she had finished her book tour, when Kate said to me, "I don't want to talk about the adoption anymore. I wrote a book. I told my story. It was hard for me. I would love it if we could just talk about science and history and the world. Could we do that?"

I understood. It was a big ask for a person like me who processes her feelings by talking about them endlessly; nevertheless, I got it. I felt the mind behind that simple ask, and that mind spoke a thousand words. I knew then, out of respect for this woman who gave birth to me and went through tremendous effort to get to this very moment of our lives, I would honor her request. It was time for me to move into a new kind of relationship with her, one where the fact that she had given me up for adoption was no longer the focal point of our connection. My choice was to move forward, sharing as much love as I possibly could, birthing a new story with Kate in this lifetime.

Of course, I will continue to process my own inner world as an adoptee, since there is no other option for me but to do so. As long as I live and breathe, I need to face my primal wound, own it, accept it, and love it as part of my journey in this life. I do this for my awakening, for my peace, and for being able to authentically support others with wounds like mine.

Part Two

" *Go within yourself;*
everything begins with you. "

—Ilchi Lee

My True Self,
My Absolute Value

Much of my life's struggle has come from misbelieving that the emotions I felt, the way others treated me, and the way I hurt, were a testament to my value, my worth. I believed in what my "stories" told me about myself.

We all have our stories. I am talking about the unconscious ones that grow like weeds from the deep wounds of our lives, stories layered upon stories that color our perspectives, that affect our relationship with those close to us, with the world at large and, most seriously, with ourselves.

From a very young age, I experienced an extreme sense of jealousy toward other children—always comparing myself to them and evaluating my worth against what I considered their worth to be.

The first and worst memory I have of doing so was when Joey O'Grady's name was pulled for a raffle during a school-wide assembly. I felt a twinge of jealousy as I watched my kindergarten classmate walk onto the stage to receive his Candy Land board game. How I wished it could have been me! I didn't even know what to call this feeling, as I had never experienced it before, so I shrugged it off.

However, the feeling escalated exponentially when I returned to my classroom to find all the other children, as well as my teacher, crowded around Joey, cheering and congratulating him. The feeling was so overwhelming I couldn't even enter the room. I just watched through the narrow, rectangular window on the side of the door, my insides wrenching. I felt frozen, nearly blinded by jealousy. My five-year-old world had turned black.

When my teacher looked over and caught my eye, I ran off to the bathroom to hide. Huddled by the radiator next to the stalls, I cried and cried, completely humiliated. Because Joey had won and I had lost, because he had gotten all the attention and I had not, I felt there was something unforgivably wrong with me. I even felt I didn't deserve to be alive. I was devastated.

This is my first memory of self-hatred.

I have looked back on that moment many times along my journey, wondering where that deeply tortured feeling had come from at such a young age. How could I have interpreted Joey O'Grady's win with so much pain? I have taken this incident apart again and again because that same feeling has reared its ugly head on many more occasions over the course of my life than I care to count—in relationships, in the face of failure, and at times, even in front of others' good fortunes.

That self-hatred was a ball and chain, and I was its prisoner.

Ultimately, my pain was not about Joey O'Grady; it was all about me. My paralyzing sense of shame and intense lack of self-worth triggered an instinct to sabotage myself. All I could do with the weight of that pain was to project it onto others. It was easier to say, "I'm jealous of *you*," than to feel the ache of it in my own heart. Such pain drove me into misery, as I felt hopeless to resolve it.

Finally, through years of practice, I was able to take off my shame-colored glasses long enough to catch a glimpse of a new perspective. I was able to realize that this feeling had *nothing* to do with the situations I found myself in *nor* the people in them.

It was my own story—one that had been hiding deep within me and had made its appearance on that day in kindergarten. It was a story built on a belief that grew in my bones, a belief that I shouldn't exist. It was a deep and excruciating story that I was not wanted, that I did not belong here on this earth, and that, somehow, even the earth itself didn't want me. Any sort of life situation, small or big, that showed others as better or more fortunate than I, in any way, proved my belief was true.

No one ever *told* me this story; that's why it was hard to identify. My parents were only kind and loving to me. They showered me with praises and hugs, but once I was away from the safety of their arms, this story took hold of me and did not let go.

I was the one who needed to do the letting go. This story wasn't real. *It was just a story*—one I was attached to, that I was *addicted* to, that distorted the way I saw myself and the way I interpreted the world around me.

However, this story has never had anything to do with who I *really* am. Before I ever defined myself by this story, before I was ever the identity of Danielle Gaudette, or even "Baby Mulgrew," I was a pure soul. That pure soul is valuable in and of itself. It cannot be compared to others; it cannot be damaged or destroyed. There is absolutely nothing that can threaten it.

That pure soul has value and worth—just as it is.

In my study of universal principles, I came across a passage that says this so well.

> Having been hurt greatly, many people think only and constantly of those hurts. Holding onto your hurt doesn't heal it. The past has passed, the future is yet to come. Those who know Absolute Value laugh out loud. "It rained on me," they say with a laugh, and shrug it off. It's not always raining. Sooner or later the rain stops, and, eventually, the sun comes out again. Those who know Absolute Value can create their lives anew. —Ilchi Lee

What is Absolute Value? To use the above example, the sun would be the Absolute Value. It is always shining in the sky; it's just that clouds come and temporarily cover it, or the earth turns and temporarily hides it from us. However, it is always there, brilliantly shining and waiting. It doesn't get sad or upset when it's covered. It just shines in its self-existent way.

Just like the sun, my true nature shines—bright, unbreakable, and unending. It may get shrouded from time to time with the stormy weather of my heart, but it is always there.

When I can remember that *this* is my value—not the rain nor the wind of my thoughts, emotions, and wounds, but this eternally shining light—then I can allow my pain to pass through me like mist.

We can call this light, the light of our soul, or the light of our divinity, or the light of oneness. What we call it is not important. Finding it and feeling this Absolute Value is what's meaningful.

From the moment we do so, we can begin to cultivate ourselves to *live* as this value, *creating our lives anew.*

Self-Mastery

work hard to create myself anew, to heal and cultivate myself. It's a process.

After my blissful meeting with my soul at the Finding True Self workshop, it wasn't as if I was suddenly "enlightened." I had gotten a taste of my Absolute Value, but it was just the beginning. Through that experience, I realized that I had been living in an upside-down house, that I had finally found the door to get out of it, but that door was on the ceiling! It was my job to climb up and out, and to begin living my new life. The steps to make that climb—where to put my feet and reach with my hands—were inside the principles of Brain Education.

Brain Education, created by Ilchi Lee, is the curriculum upon which Body & Brain practice is based. It's about the health of the body, mind, and spirit. Ultimately, it's about the health of society and the earth. It begins with training our bodies, our ki-energy systems, and our brains to become healthy, happy, peaceful, productive, and creative.[1]

I was intrigued by Brain Education because it gave me concrete principles and practices to become my True Self—not just

---

1 For an official description of the five steps of Brain Education, please visit www.ilchi.com/teachings.

to find my True Self, not just to feel it once or twice, but to *become* it. This is the journey I so wanted to take, the journey I *chose* to take—the journey of a lifetime.

There were moments in the beginning of that journey, not long after Matt had left for the farm and I was living alone, practicing every day, that I would get so frustrated. I struggled with the size of the gap between the possibility I felt inside my soul, and the person I was day-to-day. When I closed my eyes and looked inside, there was a brightly shining light of peace— perfect in and of itself. When I opened my eyes and tried to maintain that feeling as I lived in the world, I became even less tolerant of every little bit of annoyance I felt, every bit of sadness, every bit of fear. Next to the pure light, my emotions now appeared uglier to me, the way the tiniest bit of dirt might stand out as filth tarnishing a flawlessly white surface. There was even a day when I was so crazed that I threw a pot across the kitchen, shouting at my own emotion, "No! I only want to feel my True Self! Go away!"

Tangled in self-judgment, I was overcome with the feeling that it was more painful to *taste* the possibility that lay within me and not be able to live it than to not know it at all.

The more I agonized over closing this gap, the more sincerely I practiced. Although I was a disciplined practitioner, I was also a complicated one. At any given moment, my emotions were so strong, my preconceptions so deep, and my wounds just a hair's width below the surface.

Early on, I was fortunate enough to meet a mentor who understood my sensitivity. She showed me how to break down the five steps of Brain Education into eight smaller steps. They became a set of simple tools that, at first, I used almost every minute of the day. These tools enabled me to put Brain Education into practice in a whole new way.

These eight smaller steps were so helpful to me that many years later, as a trainer, I created a weekly course based on them. Designed to help students develop their awareness and transform their habits, this course is called Self-Mastery. The goal is the same as that of Brain Education: becoming the master of yourself and your life.

We all want to master ourselves. No one likes feeling helpless, hopeless, or out of control. The Self-Mastery steps provided me with so much awakening, clarity, and empowerment that I wanted to offer this healing tool to others who struggle with themselves the way I have. I wanted to illustrate, through my own personal experience, the transformations possible through each step.

For those who get in their own way, for those who are too hard on themselves, for those who are looking for hope, my wish is that these eight steps of Self-Mastery will provide a foothold.

The Eight Steps of Self-Mastery

1. Awaken—stimulate your physical body strongly enough to bring your mind back into your body.
2. Feel—feel everything honestly.
3. Watch—identify all your feelings without judgment.
4. Accept—embrace all parts of yourself with ownership.
5. Choose—choose for your True Self.

6. Act—take action that aligns with your choice.
7. Evaluate—set a goal, then awaken, feel, watch, accept, and choose again for that goal.
8. Create—create yourself and your life as you really want it to be.

Awaken

*T*o begin mastering ourselves, we must first bring our awareness from the outer world back to our inner world—bring
our minds back to our bodies. To do that, we need to
stimulate our physical bodies with mindful exercise—exercise
that attracts the mind to the feeling in the body. It could be
walking, jogging, stretching, or something more energetic like
body tapping, bowing, or simply breathing.[2] It could even be
strength training, as long as it's done mindfully.

Through our mindful exercise, we start to *awaken our inner
senses*, and our minds are pulled inward, deeper and deeper, by
those senses. Whatever exercise works best for each of us will
do. What's important is that we need to keep exercising until we
quiet our busy thoughts and pull our scattered awareness back
to the simple sensations of the body.

My favorite training for bringing my mind back to my body
is Body & Brain's signature exercise, Dahn Jon tapping. It was
the first exercise that let me really experience the power of the
lower Dahn Jon. The Korean words *Dahn Jon* literally mean
"energy center." The lower Dahn Jon refers to the energy center
of the physical body, the area of the second chakra. Consistently

---

2   See daniellegaudette.com for Body & Brain TV energy exercise videos.

tapping on this part of my body has helped me transform my relationship with my emotional world.

The lower Dahn Jon refers to the area about 1.5 inches below your belly button. If you place three fingers on your abdomen, putting your forefinger on your navel, the point underneath your ring finger will have you in the right spot, the area just above your bladder. Now, if you imagine the place another 1.5 inches inward, that is the Dahn Jon.

Dahn Jon tapping rhythmically stimulates this part of the body. Make a tight fist, lead with the pinky-side and tap the Dahn Jon in an alternating fashion.[3] As you tap repetitively, the sensation in this area begins to wake up.

For many people, the lower Dahn Jon feels quite numb at first, so it's hard to understand why anyone would "hit" themselves there. We are using our fists to stimulate the energy center, not to cause any pain. The purpose of this exercise is to awaken both the physical sensations and the energy sensations that have lain dormant.

It took time for me to discover the real power of Dahn Jon tapping. My best friend, Genia, and I were interning together at a Body & Brain Center in Newton, Massachusetts. We were learning how to run the center under our mentor's guidance. Genia's personality was strong and sharp back then, mine was soft and sensitive. This difference made us great friends, but, in that particular moment of my life, I found myself reacting emotionally to her and losing my inner center. In her sharp moments,

---

3   See daniellegaudette.com for a Body & Brain TV video on Dahn Jon tapping.

I would start to doubt myself, and all sorts of incessant worries would arise. My mentor became aware of this and recommended that I tap my Dahn Jon 3,000 times a day, every day, until I could recover my centeredness. As a diligent student, desperate to get out from under the grip of my anxiety, I followed her advice.

I started tapping my Dahn Jon throughout the day and keeping count: one hundred Dahn Jon taps while brushing my teeth, one thousand Dahn Jon taps while driving to the center. I found it to be so grounding. Nothing else could bring me to such a state of calm and clarity. As my abdomen got warmer, the busyness in my head would slowly quiet, and the nervousness bursting through my chest would slide down and dissolve into my belly. I started to feel my Dahn Jon as a living creature that I could feed my negative thoughts and emotions to, and it would eat them up, converting them into power. By the time I got to 3,000 each day, I felt a warm sense of fullness and strength within. All those thoughts and emotions were just energy being transformed into vitality in my core.

I tapped my Dahn Jon 3,000 times every day for three months. My Dahn Jon became the seat belt I needed to buckle up in order to keep myself safe and steady through my heart's wild and bumpy ride. I realized my Dahn Jon was like medicine inside my body—inside all of our bodies—that just needed to be awakened through sincere and consistent stimulation. Once I awakened that sense, there was no duplication for the feeling of deep and complete acceptance of all things in that cozy, quiet but full, centered place within.

This is Self-Mastery step one—Awaken.[4]

Recommended Training for Awaken

Give it a try!

1. Stand with your feet shoulder-width apart.
2. Bend your knees.
3. Tilt your pelvis forward, tucking your tailbone.
4. Keep your spine straight.
5. Lower your chin slightly.
6. Relax your shoulders.
7. Exhale through your mouth.
8. Make tight fists, lead with the pinky-side, and stimulate your Dahn Jon in an alternating fashion.
9. Start by tapping 100 times.

After getting a feel for it, try tapping your Dahn Jon for five minutes each day, paying attention to the sensations in your body and mind.

---

4   Awaken is part of Brain Education step #1: Brain Sensitizing.

Feel

*O*nce our minds have come back to our bodies, we need to *honestly feel everything* that's going on inside us. When we try to do that, we find a myriad of feelings and sensations. Sometimes, we might feel warm, relaxing, comfortable sensations; other times, we might feel tension, stuffiness, heaviness, or even negative emotions that have been lurking within. The purpose of this step is to just *feel* all of it.

As we begin the process, we may experience resistance and self-protection. A voice inside might argue, "Why would I want to feel all these uncomfortable feelings?" That's understandable. We have been enculturated to believe that feeling either physical or emotional pain is somehow "bad," so we keep trying to look away from it—avoiding it and numbing ourselves. This often leads us to feel insecure, disconnected, and even lost. If we want to find answers to our problems, solutions to our hurts, power to overcome our inner struggles, and the light that shines on the other side of it all, we need to go within, to feel inside ourselves.

It may seem counterintuitive to *feel into* sensations that cause discomfort, but there is an important energy principle at work here: where the mind goes, energy follows. If we bring our minds to the pain, healing energy will flow there and begin to break up the stagnation and blockages that have caused such pain. Energy healing happens when we feel.

Sinking into a feeling, relaxing, and going deeper into it requires courage. We need courage to allow our minds to come out from *thinking about* the feeling and *enter into* the feeling. We develop that courage by practicing awakening exercises regularly.

After I had discovered the power of Dahn Jon tapping, it became my favorite awakening exercise. I would take time every day to tap for twenty minutes, processing my feelings by simply feeling them. As I tapped, I began to sort out the tangled mess of emotions inside me by allowing myself to feel them honestly.

There were times when I could not overcome my mind's grip on my incessant thoughts and emotions. I could not allow the energy that was stuck in my head to come down into my Dahn Jon, no matter how long I tapped. In that state, I had no choice but to admit those feelings to myself *out loud*, one by one, as if I was taking inventory. This practice helped me stay present and be completely honest with myself.

This exercise became like writing in a diary. It was my time to speak all my feelings to myself with full disclosure. "I feel, worried, worried, worried. I feel angry, angry, angry. I feel scared, scared, scared." The more I would calmly repeat these feelings to myself, the more they would ease.

I started to realize that it was my feelings about my feelings that were causing the biggest problem for me. I was anxious that I was anxious, angry for being angry, and scared that I was scared. I was sad that I was sad and worried about being so worried all the time. I had been living in a state of self-blame and disappointment, and it was wearing me out.

When I finally gave myself permission to feel each and every feeling, my mind started to release its grip. I found that feeling one emotion at a time, without the other emotions piled up on top, started to become manageable. Simply being worried—rather than worried that I was worried—was something I could handle. Soon, my insides began to relax.

I practiced nonstop for weeks at a time. Beyond my twenty minutes of daily tapping and talking, whenever an emotion would come up and overwhelm me in my daily life, I just kept repeating it out loud to myself.

There was one week when I felt drenched in anxiety from head to toe, so I simply said, quietly to myself, "I feel anxious, anxious, anxious." I would be running errands, or cleaning the dishes, or eating my lunch, and I just kept facing my feeling. "I feel anxious, anxious, anxious." Instead of asking, "*Why* do I feel anxious?" then getting even more anxious about it, I just stated the feeling again and again.

At some moment, it was as if my brain gave up, let go of the fight with the feeling, and completely allowed the feeling to just *be*. When that happened, I felt a peace that reminded me of sitting on the bank of my imaginary river, watching all the colored boats flow by. This peace spread throughout my entire chest, opening my heart. All the cells in my body seemed to be recalibrating to this new feeling. From within this new peaceful sensation arose a voice that comforted me, "I feel anxiety, and it's okay. It's okay."

I saw my mentor at the end of that week, and she looked

at me with surprise. She tilted her head at the sight of my face, looked into my eyes, then picked up my hands and looked at my palms. "Oh," she said happily, "you fought a big war with your anxiety this week! And you won!"

I smiled. The fist-like knot that had perpetually squeezed my heart whenever I would spiral into an anxious episode had softened. After that, any time that knot tightened again, I just repeated my feeling over and over, until it melted. I had discovered the healing power of feeling my feelings.

This is step two—Feel.[5]

Recommended Training for Feel

If you have been tapping your Dahn Jon regularly for five minutes, try to extend the time up to the baseline recommendation of twenty minutes. Once you have tapped your Dahn Jon for twenty minutes, you will be able to experience a deeper energetic shift.

1. Tap your Dahn Jon continuously for up to twenty minutes.
2. Speak out all the feelings that rise to your awareness from your body and mind. You don't have to think about your feelings. If you are not aware of any feelings, just breathe out.
3. Fill in the blank of the following sentence, **"I allow myself to feel_____."** It may be physical, such as, "I allow myself to feel stiffness, achiness, pain, heat." It may be emotional, such as, "I allow myself to feel angry, frustrated, sad, anxious."

---

5   Feel is also part of Brain Education step #1: Brain Sensitizing.

4. Give yourself permission to feel fully. Speak freely and honestly, expressing yourself to yourself.

Note: Even no feeling, lack of feeling, or numbness are still feelings. If you find yourself experiencing these, the key is to feel into the nothingness, the lack, the numbness. Try to feel deeper into those weak sensations, rather than being put off by them or giving up.

Watch

*O*nce we start feeling our feelings, the next step is to observe them, or *watch* them. Watching means to identify our feelings without judgment.

When I say, "I feel anxious, anxious, anxious," I'm already watching. I'm feeling the sensation in my body, naming it as anxiety, and if I am able, I'm not judging that emotion as negative, nor am I judging myself for having it. Watching is different from mental examination or analysis, both of which naturally involve judgment. Because our minds are habituated to judge, it's not easy to stop this way of thinking. That's why we need to feel first—there is no true watching without having our minds rooted in the feeling of our bodies.

As I've already mentioned, most people have the strong belief that negative feelings are "bad" and positive feelings are "good," so dropping into our feelings can be challenging. It's almost instinctual to react to negative feelings, escaping them through avoidance. Some of us avoid by hopping right back into thoughts and ideas about a feeling; others avoid with distractions like entertainment, alcohol, food, or friends; still others avoid facing their honest feelings by creating even more emotion, more drama, and more unnecessary pain. All these ways of avoiding are reactions that involve judgment or blame toward the self, others, or both. It's important to remember that reacting is the opposite of watching.

We react because we identify with our feelings too much. This false identification may be conscious or unconscious, but it's ingrained in each of us, passed down through generations. We keep wrongly believing that we *are* our thoughts, we *are* our emotions, and we *are* the information we have accumulated from a lifetime of experience. But we are none of those things. The bottom line is that we have lost our true identity, our True Self.

This is precisely why watching is so important. We must create separation between who we *really* are (our True Self) and who we *think* we are (our thoughts, emotions, beliefs). Every time we create even a little bit of space between who we really are and who we think we are, we get out of the grip of the false identities and begin to catch a sense that this feeling is just a feeling, this emotion is just an emotion, and it's not who we really are. Once we cultivate the ability to observe ourselves from a distance, we liberate ourselves from living as slaves to our false inner programming.

Steps 1 and 2 of Self-Mastery work together. We must feel to watch, and we must watch to feel more deeply. Feeling into the emotion and calling it what it is, such as, "I feel fear," is a helpful tool. However, it's even more helpful to say what the truth of the matter is: "I have the feeling of fear inside, but it's not who I really am."

The moment we say that to ourselves, we begin conscious separation. Instead of being consumed by the feeling of being afraid, we recognize that fear is just a feeling we have inside, one among many feelings, but it is not our True Self. In fact, it is our True Self, our soul-power, that strengthens each time we say, "I see you, my emotion. I hear you, I feel you, but you are not me." This is a good sentence to use with Dahn Jon tapping or any awakening exercise. It is not only comforting but also healthy and empowering to train ourselves to recognize that we are not our feelings.

In recent months, I have taken to using this tool to feel and watch myself when I breathe. It is especially effective if I have discomfort in my body. For example, if I worry too much, I can experience pain in my stomach. When that happens, I sit in half-lotus posture, straighten my spine, bring my ten fingertips together as if I were holding a ball, and rest them in my lap. This is an awakening posture that I sometimes use for bringing my mind back to my body. Then, I sit quietly and watch.

Rather than wrestle with the discomfort in my stomach, rather than react to it with frustration and more worried thoughts about it, I just allow my awareness to rest on the pain, and I breathe. Instead of trying to "fix" the pain, I just let it be. I remind myself from time to time, *This pain is not me, it's just a feeling I have inside.* Sometimes, I even speak that sentence out loud, quietly to myself, removing any of the random judgments or meaning-making that my mind likes to do when I try to relax into the discomfort. As I do, I find all kinds of feelings come up. Pain tangled with worries, stress, and a desire to control things that I have no control over twist my upper abdomen into a knot. Instead of trying to block, suppress, or avoid this incredibly uncomfortable twisting feeling, instead of freaking out that perhaps there is something seriously wrong with my stomach (which the fearful, paranoid part of my mind would have me believe), I just keep feeling and identifying those feelings without adding any judgment. "I have the feeling of worry inside, but worry is not me. I have the desire to control, but the desire to control is not me."

The more I can hold my mind steady in the painful area of my body, the more the pain dissipates. By the end of twenty minutes, I am left feeling relief in my stomach, warmth in my Dahn Jon, and clarity in my brain. When I stop reacting, when I make the effort to separate from identifying with my feelings and simply observe myself, healing occurs.

There is no need for me to be afraid of my own feelings. No matter how old they are, how deep they feel, what kind of wounds they stir, how dark they may seem, they are not real. I am confident about this. I simply have not yet mastered them all.

Therefore, the deeper ones, the ones I haven't yet been able to take a complete look at, still bite me sometimes, and sometimes their bite is worse than at other times. But again, these are ghost bites—old memories, old beliefs, twisted perceptions. They are not the truth of me. They do not speak of my Absolute Value, and I'm pretty tired from a lifetime of giving them power.

To have the strength to feel our feelings accurately and watch them without judging them, we train ourselves. Overcoming ourselves and developing self-mastery involves quite a bit of discomfort, but there is a reward of freedom at the end! It takes practice, daily practice, even hourly and moment-to-moment practice, to stay awake, aware, and alert.

This is step three—Watch.[6]

Recommended Training for Watch

1. Tap your Dahn Jon continuously for up to twenty minutes.
2. Speak out all the feelings in your body that rise to your awareness using the following sentences: "**I have the feeling of____ but ____ is not me.**" Or, "**I have____ inside of me. ____ is not who I really am.**"
3. Be careful not to get caught up in thoughts or judgments. If you do, patiently bring your awareness back to the feeling that you have in your body.

Through repeating the sentences, try to catch the sense of making space between you and the feeling. Even if you can get only a tiny bit of distance between you and the feeling, it will bring you some relief.

---

6   Watch is a part of Brain Education step #2: Brain Versatilizing.

Accept

The eight steps to Self-Mastery have an order, but, as I mentioned, Feel and Watch work together. Accept, the fourth step, is closely tied in as well, making the three steps go hand in hand. If we can fully sink into the feeling, we are automatically watching the feeling. If we are truly watching with no judgment, we are automatically accepting the feeling.

However, if we struggle deeply with accepting ourselves, if we are too hard on ourselves, too critical of any "negative" aspect of ourselves—from our pain to our thoughts, to our emotions, to our beliefs—we might find it difficult to watch those feelings, or we might cut ourselves off from feeling altogether. In those cases, we need to practice a little bit of acceptance first.

Accept can be divided in two parts. Part 1 is for those who struggle with allowing themselves to feel or to watch their feelings because they are too hard on themselves. For them, *cultivating a loving relationship with themselves* must come first. Part 2 is for those who have practiced self-love enough to feel ready to *take ownership of the whole of their inner landscape.*

Accept, Part 1—Cultivating a Loving Relationship with Oneself

I was the kind of person who wrestled with all my feelings, unable to truly "watch" any of them, until I could catch a little breath of self-acceptance. In order to catch that breath, I needed to have many healing conversations with myself. I would often have these conversations while engaged in an exercise Body & Brain calls Whole Body Tapping. I would literally tap my body with fists or open palms, feeling the sensations and bringing my mind inward.[7]

As a catalyst for helping me sink into these internal conversations, I would use the sentence, "I forgive myself." Other sentences could have worked just as well, such as, "I'm sorry to myself for feeling angry, feeling anxious, feeling whatever," or "I allow myself to feel pain in my stomach, pain in my hip, or pain wherever, and it's okay."

I chose the phrase, "I forgive myself," because each time I said it, I felt its powerful healing effect. Tapping all over, I would forgive myself for any uncomfortable feeling that arose. Specifically, I would say, "I forgive myself for having tension in my chest; I forgive myself for thinking too much; I forgive myself for being tired." Without judging or analyzing any of this, without getting caught up in the question of whether or not I *really* forgave myself for those things, I would just speak freely and openly while feeling my body. I found that the more

---

7   See daniellegaudette.com for a Body & Brain TV video on Whole Body Tapping.

I voiced my forgiveness, the more I could relax and let go, and the more a feeling of gratitude and love began to flow within me.

I discovered that I was living in annoyance with myself about a lot of little things. Forgiving myself for those annoyances lifted a huge weight, and what remained was a natural sense of okayness. The more sincerely I spoke to each part of myself, the more I found deeper feelings rising for forgiveness: "I forgive myself for having the feeling of being weak; I forgive myself for having the feeling that I never get things right; I forgive myself for having the feeling of not being enough." As I diligently and sincerely continued with this exercise, I felt a great relief—like a child who has confessed her secret wrongdoings to her mother and has received a loving "It's all right, honey" embrace from her. It was healing to discover the me within that could forgive myself.

Once I was able to forgive myself even a *tiny* bit for *some* of my feelings, my watching practice started working. I had caught the sense of how to relinquish my self-judgment, even if just for a moment. I was now ready for the second step in accepting: taking ownership.

Accept, Part 2—Taking Ownership of One's Whole Inner Landscape

We are all busy people. We are busy taking care of our families, our jobs, our responsibilities. As we live our lives, our consciousness is directed outward, toward others. Maintaining this outward consciousness for a prolonged period, without turning inward for sincere self-reflection, causes us to easily become victims of the world around us. Because of what we read or hear on social media, what our friends and loved ones say or do, even what the weather does, we find ourselves unhappy.

No matter how hard we try, we cannot change what we read or hear on social media; we cannot change the way people in our lives behave; we cannot change the weather. If our happiness must rely on these external conditions, we can never be happy, because we have put our happiness in the hands of others, relinquishing our power to create it ourselves, becoming victims of circumstance. If, without our realizing it, this becomes a habit, eventually our overall sense of well-being will become negatively impacted.

To break this habit, we must recognize that we have become enslaved by the victim mentality we all have within us. We need to accept, to embrace this victim mentality, and take ownership of it. Doing so is the beginning of changing the only thing we *can* change—ourselves.

This does not mean we should allow ourselves to be treated inappropriately. However, before we respond to another's unhealthy behavior, it's important for us to first accept the feelings it has caused us to feel.

Rather than blaming my unhappiness on people or circumstances outside of myself, I must recognize that everything in my life that makes me unhappy or unsettled is my own internal issue. My unhappiness stems from *my* negative thoughts, *my* negative emotions, *my* stories, *my* beliefs, *my* hurts, *my* perspectives, *my* ideas, *my* expectations, *my* opinions, *my* reactions. None of these sources of unhappiness are *me*; they are simply what I have inside

ACCEPT

of me; therefore, they are mine.

The good news is that since the source of unhappiness is mine, I am the only one who can fix it. I am the only one who can end the cycle of blaming others for my problems, my hurts, my struggles. I simply take ownership. It's important to emphasize that taking ownership is *not* the same as blaming myself. I blame myself—I punish and hurt myself—when I judge myself negatively, believing I have done something bad or wrong. This is not the meaning of taking ownership.

Ownership is nonjudgmental. It's the opposite of self-blame and faultfinding; it's *self-embracing*. It includes an element of unconditional acceptance. It's a mind that says, "Yes, I have this emotion, this habit, this pain inside, *and it's okay*. It's just a feeling. This feeling is not me, it's mine."

Once I own this feeling, once I embrace it, I release myself from it and begin to feel the sweet relief that comes with letting go. Increased energy circulation follows, and there is a sense of lightness and relaxation in my body because I have freed myself from something I had been holding on to when I was stuck in the mindset of a victim.

To make the shift from victimization to ownership, I like to use the simple sentence, "I have [insert a feeling], but [this feeling] is not me, it's mine." This sentence includes feeling the feeling, separating from the feeling, and embracing the feeling with acceptance that it's not who I *really* am, it's just a feeling, and it's mine to change anytime I want.

Using this sentence has helped me greatly in my internal healing process with Kate. When my mentor told me that I had

147

completed my work with my childhood wounds, and what was left was the work I needed to do with my biological parents, she suggested I write Kate a letter. This was one of the rare times I was not ready to follow my mentor's advice. I was not ready because there was so much I had not accepted. I was still in the place of looking outward, toward Kate. The more I looked at her, the more blame arose within me, trapping me in a state of self-victimization. It was only when I began to accept my inner landscape that the chaos of my victimization started to untangle.

I spent a lot of time tapping my Dahn Jon, speaking out loud, "My sadness is not me, it's mine; my anger is not me, it's mine; my feeling of rejection is not me, it's mine; my guilt is not me, it's mine." I would even walk around my house doing chores on a Sunday afternoon, talking it all out quietly to myself, embracing everything I felt in my heart.

I still practice this step of acceptance diligently each day. Ever since I could not bring myself to write a letter to Kate, this practice has been especially transformative in the healing work I have been doing. I have found it is no longer necessary to make my hurts about her because they are just my own reactions and responses.

I especially noticed this transformation one of the last times I saw her. I was sitting across the table from her at a restaurant, as I often do, but this time, several family members had gathered to celebrate the day after Alec's wedding. Kate and Alec were sitting side-by-side, involved in a playful, yet intimate, chat. I was observing how close they had become over the years and perhaps felt a bit of envy. I looked around and became aware that everyone else at the table was also engaged in jovial conversation, except for me. Suddenly, I felt extremely left out. A massive wave of darkness washed over me. I was falling into the deep hole that lives in the sidewalk of my heart—a hole of insecurity, humiliation, and shame. All I could do in that awkward moment was realize it, feel it, and talk it out with myself. As a seasoned practitioner, I had enough awareness to know that, although I was in pain, this situation was an opportunity.

Okay, I said to myself, *this is my hole, and I'm the only one who can get myself out of it. What is it that I'm actually feeling in this hole? I feel a feeling of not-enoughness. Beyond that, I feel bad that I'm not enough.*

"I'm bad that I'm not enough" was such a familiar feeling to me. Because I had been processing my feelings for so long, feeling them, being honest with myself about them, I was immediately able to recognize this feeling as guilt. It was the usual feeling that arose from believing that, because I'm being rejected at this moment, I must not be enough in some way. Since I'm not enough, I must have done something wrong, and now I feel guilty about whatever it is I have done.

Ah, this is my guilt! Okay, my guilt, I feel you, but you are not me, you are mine. I have guilt inside me, but I am not my guilt. Guilt, you are not me, you are mine.

After repeating this a few times to myself, I felt the darkness lift, and a lightness came over me. I had fully taken ownership of my own feeling, and it had brought a sweet breeze of acceptance into my heart. I looked around once more and saw that everything was perfectly okay. We were all having a lovely celebration, and I could easily turn to the people on my left or on my right at any moment and jump into the conversation. It was as if I had new eyes to see the same scenario in a completely different light. I looked across the table again and felt sincerely joyful to see Kate and Alec looking so happy. This was a beautiful moment that my guilt almost stole from me; but because I was able to own it, I was able to do something about it. My ability to do that in one of my most delicate and vulnerable situations, after years of practicing and failing many times, was a great achievement, and I finished that evening feeling proud of myself.

I had experienced such a deep level of acceptance that it empowered me to realize something important: despite what has happened to me in this life—how I have interpreted it, how I have held on to it, how I have made a thousand stories and meanings about it—my response to all of it is mine, and mine alone, to claim. It is mine and mine alone to change.

This is step four—Accept.[8]

Recommended Training for Accept

For Self-Forgiveness:

1. Tap freely, all over the body, for up to twenty minutes, using fists or open palms. Without any specific order or set routine, tap in the places that feel good, the places that feel weak or tired, and the places that hurt. Tap all over, listening to the body, breathing out, and releasing stuck energy.

2. Repeat the sentence, **"I forgive myself for_____."** Put

---

8   Accept is a part of Brain Education step #3: Brain Refreshing.

every feeling that comes up, physical or emotional, small or large, shallow or deep, into that sentence while tapping all over.

3. Keep feeling how your body and mind respond to, "I forgive myself."

For Taking Ownership:

1. Tap your Dahn Jon for up to twenty minutes.
2. Fill in the blanks for the sentence, **"I have_____; _____ is not me, it's mine."** This is a powerful sentence that will help you begin to take ownership of your feelings.
3. Once you become familiar with the feeling of relief, relaxation, or letting go that taking ownership provides, you can use this sentence as a tool to speak to yourself whenever you find yourself falling victim to your emotions.

Choose

*O*nce we truly own our feelings, we can change ourselves at any time, even in an instant, *if we so choose*. For example, if I can watch and accept my anger, then I can choose to *not* react by berating myself or saying something unkind to someone else. Instead, I can consider other choices: I can walk away, I can breathe out, or I can smile. I can even choose to try to understand the other person. There are infinite choices. Ideally, the practice is to choose what is best for my soul, my True Self, rather than to choose for my negative thoughts, emotions, and habits.

The first four steps of Self-Mastery guide us back into our bodies so that we can accept all that we have and allow ourselves to just *be*. The second four steps, starting with Choose, are what help us to take action, to *do*. Ideally, we want to get ourselves into a healthy, centered, loving state of being, then take action from that place.

The principle of choice is this: whatever we choose, grows. If we choose our love, it will grow bigger and stronger in our lives, but if we choose our fear, that emotional layer of fear will get thicker. Therefore, Choose is the step where we begin to create our lives.

To create our lives anew, we must become more *conscious*

choosers. Whether we know it or not, we are choosing something every moment. If we don't watch ourselves closely, we might make unconscious habitual choices from our emotions, excuses, beliefs, justifications, judgments, and self-victimization. It's important to become aware that when we unknowingly make such choices, we sleepwalk through our lives.

The power is completely in our hands. If there is a change we want to make, we begin by making a healthier choice. Every moment we have a new chance to choose again. Even if we unconsciously fell into our emotions and victim mentality last week, yesterday, five minutes or fifty years ago, we can choose again, right now, for something different. That is the power of being a human being, and there is nothing and no one outside ourselves who can stop us from exercising that power.

The question is, what do I want to choose for? What do I really want?

Personally, I really want to choose for my soul. I want to choose for growing my soul's light. My choice is clear, although I am not always able to follow through, which is why I am practicing, at the very least, to stay conscious of myself as much as I can. Fortunately, life itself gives me a lot of opportunities!

One morning, sitting at my kitchen table, eating my oatmeal, I experienced the transformative power of awakening, feeling, watching, accepting, and choosing. My phone buzzed, and I looked down to find a group chat text from a colleague with whom I had a difficult relationship. Upon seeing her name, a huge rush of heat came shooting up from my chest to my face, and I felt a surge of emotion. *Oh,* I thought to myself, *this is serious. I'd better work on this right now.* I put my phone down, I put my spoon down, and right there, at the breakfast table, I decided to feel.

I closed my eyes and exhaled to release some of the heat and to quiet my reactive mind. I brought my mind, my awareness, into the feeling of my body. Because I had been practicing these techniques for many years, I was able to do so without needing to tap, just by riding the rhythm of my breathing to bring my mind inward. The first feeling I was able to identify was anger. *No,* I thought, *this is more than anger.*

As I felt *into* my anger, I realized that it was actually a feeling of hate.

I understand that most people have a lot of preconceptions and judgments about hate. "It's *bad* to hate. I'm *bad* if I feel hate toward someone. I want to always be a good and kind person to all."

If I had not been able to watch myself, I, too, would have gotten stuck in judgment about hate that morning. If I had, I wouldn't have allowed myself to fully feel it. If I had resisted the feeling that was occurring, if I had been unable to accept it as it was, I would never have been able to *choose* to go beyond it, to discover what was on the other side.

So, I bravely allowed myself to sink into the center of my hate. When I did that, I felt that inside my hate, there was a feeling of hurt. It felt as though the root of my hate came from my hurt. I wondered if perhaps this was the root of all the hate and anger in this world—unprocessed hurt—hurt that one is not able to own. It's my hurt, just like it's my hate and my anger. It's my choice to hurt.

As I felt my hurt, my colleague came to mind once more. She, too, may have had some kind of hurt deep inside her own heart. Our unresolved issue may have stemmed from such reciprocal feelings. Her hurt hurt me; my hurt hurt her back. Considering that possibility, my hurt transformed into empathy, and I felt my heart fill with compassion and a sense of brightness.

However, my positive wave of feeling dipped, and I found myself sinking into yet another uncomfortable feeling.

As I let my awareness drop deeper, I discovered the feeling of hate was there again. *Aha, hate! I know you!* I thought. *I already know that you are just a product of my hurt, so let me choose to feel into that hurt more deeply.*

Relaxing, I gathered my courage once more and felt into the center of my hurt. It wasn't easy, as I found the energy sensation to be so very tight and dark and lacking. This lack was what was causing pain in my heart.

I tried to let my awareness enter into the lack and found that this was the place inside me that was void of love, a place where I did not allow love in, a place where I had starved myself of my own love. *Ah, all my hurt comes from a lack of love, a place where I do not love myself!* Accepting this realization, a sense of unconditional love opened inside my heart, like the morning sunlight shining in as the curtain is slowly drawn.

Finally, I had faced my hurt head-on and found an everlasting love I was ignoring, a love that was at the bottom of all my hurts. That love was always there, waiting for me to choose it. It was not love from somebody else; it was my own love, a self-existent love, emanating from my True Self, my soul. It was there waiting for me to feel in every breath, in every blue sky, in every person's heart. It was my love to feel, my love to choose, my love to share. All the times in my life I had suffered were because I had closed the door on that love and had been left shivering in the darkness of the lack.

Even when I feel hurt by another, if I look deeply enough, I can see my hurt is born from my love and care for that person, *and* from my interpretation that, somehow, they are not loving me back in the same way. This is just my perception.

The truth at the bottom of my heart is this: I have loved that person all along. It is not about what they did or did not do, said or did not say. It's about recognizing that, in the fibers of my being, I am love.

If I had not taken time to process my feelings, I may have had a bitter day filled with unnecessary arguments and agitations. Instead, upon reconnecting with this love at the breakfast table, I was able to choose love for my day. I was able to live a bright and joyful day with a greater sense of compassion as I interacted with my world.

When I allow myself to feel my feelings honestly and with courage, I bring my awareness deeper and deeper within, and the healing process begins to unfold. From there, I can watch without judgment and practice embracing everything I have with acceptance. If I do not allow myself to feel the so-called negative feelings that my ego fights with, I will miss the chance to feel the brilliance of my soul—the chance to choose my bright love.

This is step five—Choose.[9]

Recommended Training for Choose

1. Awaken: Tap your Dahn Jon for twenty minutes.
2. Feel: Feel all the feelings arising within.
3. Watch and Accept: Identify the feelings inside, recognizing they are not you, and owning them with the sentence, "**I have_____. _____ is not me, it's mine.**"
4. Choose: Practice choosing to move your awareness to the sensation of your Dahn Jon. This will help ground you, neutralize your feelings, and give you strength to make the choice for what you really want, such as increased health, happiness, or love.
5. The entire sequence looks like this: "**I have_____. _____ is not me, it's mine. I choose to feel my Dahn Jon. What do I want for my True Self?**" Try not to search for the answer to the question, "What do I want for my True Self?" Instead, speak it out like a mantra, feeling the sensations in your body transforming. If the answer arises spontaneously from your heart, feel how that feels. If not, just keep repeating the exercise.

---

9 Choose is part of Brain Education step #4: Brain Integrating.

Act

fter making a choice, it's important to follow through with an action that is in alignment with that choice.

Actions are the real choices. What we *do* is what we *really want*. Let's say we want to get fit, so we decide to get up at 7:00 a.m. every day to work out. However, when the alarm goes off in the morning, we just can't get out of bed. We snooze and snooze until we have to jump up and get ready for the day, forgoing our workout. We could make excuses like, "Oh, I was tired, and it was dark out, and my bed was so cozy," or, we could just be honest with ourselves. The truth is we *chose* to sleep in. When our choice to get out of bed is 100 percent, we will get up.

If we continuously don't *do* what we tell ourselves we *choose*, a gap forms inside of us. Our conscience is uncomfortable with this gap, and soon enough, all the bugs and dirt of disempowering thoughts, self-doubt, and negative emotions settle in. To avoid this, we need to make promises to ourselves and keep them; we need to do what we said we wanted to do. *And we need to do it right away!* When we delay, our brains begin to lose trust that we will do what we say, and that's when all those bugs creep in; that's when we lose trust in ourselves. Following through on our choices in a timely manner, with sincere actions, will set new habits in motion and create direction for our lives.

An action taken with a joyful mind will produce the best results. If the action feels like a chore, if we are stressed about it, we will perpetuate more stress and unhappiness. The action doesn't have to be big. We can begin simply and lightly. Let's say we want to be happier, so we decide to purchase a journal for writing down, at the end of each day, a list of ten things that made us happy. This may seem like a small measure, but if we shrug it off as unimportant, then we lose the chance to experience the power that even small actions have. When we do what we say we are going to do, we find that our hearts feel a sense of personal pride and fulfillment for having followed through on our choices. Our brains feel empowered and begin to provide us with more ideas for what we can do to continue to achieve what we want.

For the steps of Choose and Act, having a clear goal is important. To establish that goal, we answer the question: *What do I really want?* Once we have decided what we want to choose, we will know what action to take.

If we cannot get a clear answer to this question, if we are not sure what we want to choose, we need to back up a bit. The lack of being able to make a clear *choice* comes from something inside of us we are not accepting. When we cannot accept some emotion, desire, or belief, it clouds our ability to see clearly what choice to make. If we are unable to *accept* some aspect of ourselves, we need to back up, and ensure that we are watching ourselves well, that we are identifying what's going on inside of us without any judgment. If we can't see what it is we need to *watch*, then we need to back up even further and give ourselves time to *feel* into all our feelings more deeply. If we can't do that, we need to back up yet again and just start *awakening* our bodies with stimulating exercises. Like this, we can make use of the steps of Self-Mastery both forward and backward.

Since I was clear from the beginning of my journey that I wanted to live for my True Self, I sought actions that would help me strengthen my soul, as well as those that would help me overcome my ego.

One day I heard that several practitioners were gathering at the center in the evening to do 3,000-bow training. A bow is a full-body prostration, another energy exercise for bringing one's awareness inward and for purifying the body, mind, and spirit.[10]

We usually do twenty-one bows or 103 bows or, from time to time, we may do 1,000 bows. For someone who is not fit, even one bow can be difficult, so completing 1,000 bows is an intense activity. The act of doing 3,000 bows is akin to running a marathon. I had heard legends of trainers who had completed 3,000 bows, and I wanted to test myself in that way. Like them, I, too, wanted to overcome the limitations of my ego by challenging my body and mind for the purpose of strengthening my resolve to brighten my soul. At the time, I was babysitting a small boy, and, because his mother needed me that evening, I was unable to join my fellow practitioners at the center for the 3,000-bow training. I was both disappointed and envious.

That night, when I got home, I decided I would do 3,000

---

10   See daniellegaudette.com for a Body & Brain TV video on bowing.

bows by myself. Right there on the creaky wooden floor of my bedroom, starting at 10:00 p.m., I was determined to bow all night long if I had to. I rolled out my yoga mat and began.

I whizzed through the first 1,000 bows because I was young and strong and had been training every day. I felt refreshed and empowered, but I needed to take a short bathroom break. When I came back to my mat, something had changed.

As I started bowing again, my body felt like sludge. It was so heavy, every single bow felt difficult. It was my first time going beyond 1,000 bows, so the purification was deepening. My brain started to release all kinds of emotions and desires.

Fear appeared first. I lived alone in an old six-unit house in a seedy part of town, and I started to feel spooked. Every little noise I heard outside the window startled me. Usually, I'm not afraid of bugs, but suddenly, I became terrified of every tiny crawling creature that came out in the wee hours. I was so unnerved; I even began to imagine there might be ghosts lurking in the corners of my apartment.

Next, the desire to hydrate set in, as I was sweating profusely. My brain visualized myself holding a large glass of water. It seemed so real, I could practically taste it. As I brought it to my lips, it turned into ice-cold, cranberry juice. As I gulped it down, it transformed once more into the sweetest, most refreshingly crisp iced tea imaginable. From there, my mind told me that I must drive twenty minutes to Concord to jump into Walden Pond, right then, in the middle of the night. My desire to hydrate had morphed into a desire to immerse myself in a cool, refreshing body of water. My mind even tried to convince me that this was a message from Mother Earth and something I must do immediately.

As I was wrestling with this strong desire, finishing up my one thousand five-hundredth bow, the doorbell rang. It was 2:00 a.m. Shocked, I peeked through the blinds to find a man I'd never seen before, standing at my door, with a black backpack slung over his shoulder. Terrified, I bolted to the coat closet to hide. My heart was pounding, my head was spinning, and I didn't know what to do. In a panic, I crawled to grab my sweater, my wallet, and my car keys, stuffed my feet into my sneakers, ran out the back door to where my car was parked, and drove away.

I sped down the street with legs that felt like jelly and a brain that felt like Silly Putty. I drove to the local 24-hour store to buy a large can of lemon-flavored iced tea and a small notepad for my awakenings. I was going to Walden Pond.

As I was nearing the turn to get onto the highway, another part of my brain came online. It was as if half of my mind woke up from being possessed and asked, "What are you doing? Are you crazy? It's the middle of the night! You probably can't even get into Walden Pond right now. Just go back. This is ridiculous."

"No! I want to go!" the other half of my mind retorted. "It's a sign!" The two parts of my mind launched into an impassioned argument, tearing me in half. I pulled over to the side of the road to get to the bottom of this dispute. I began to shout out loud to overpower the inner noise. "What do I want? What do I really want?"

Finally, a small voice from deep inside my heart rose up. It was a tiny, nearly defeated voice, but it was crystal clear. "I just want to do 3,000 bows," it said. "I just want to finish doing what I said I was going to do." It was the voice of my will, and I knew what I had to do. I turned my car around, drove back to my house, and completed my 3,000-bow training.

That night, the remaining 1,500 bows were torture every bow of the way, and I did not finish until 10:00 a.m. It was a twelve-hour, epic event, and although my body was aching all over, I was so proud of myself for overcoming my ego and completing what I had set out to do.

The next day at the center, I heard the news that the students who were bowing together didn't make it to 3,000. They had all given up for various reasons—headaches, knee aches, emotional breakdowns, sheer exhaustion. I found them in the lobby, looking beaten, irritated, and disappointed. My mentor walked right up to me and said, "Wow, you look so bright! I see you overcame your limitations. Congratulations!"

Completing that action not only boosted my confidence but also made me feel proud of myself. I realized then that there is nothing more important for my brain and for my soul than doing what I said I would do. There is nothing more transformative than making choices for my best self and following through with determined action.

This is step six—Act.[11]

---

11   Act is part of Brain Education step #4: Brain Integrating.

Recommended Training for Act

1. Tap your Dahn Jon while asking your heart: "What do I really want?" After a few minutes, while still tapping, begin to answer your own question out loud. Trust your feeling— whatever arises from your heart, speak it out. It could be anything from, "I want to take a nap," to "I want peace." Without judgment, let it flow. Repeat this exercise for days or even weeks, until you land on something that you feel clear and certain about, something that feels right to your heart. It doesn't have to be a life-changing want, just something that makes you feel honestly happy in the moment.

2. Choose an activity that is aligned with that want. It could be an exercise, like tapping, bowing, or jogging. Alternatively, it could be an action that needs to be taken related to a project at work, improving your diet, an artistic creation, or expressing yourself through letter writing or journaling.

3. Make a goal to take that action for twenty-one days.

4. Each day, write about your experience in a journal—what you are feeling and how you are changing.

This is a very basic practice in keeping your promise to yourself.

Evaluate

While we are taking action on our choices, we can expect more obstacles to arise. To cross over these hurdles successfully, we need to be able to evaluate ourselves. Here, *evaluate* means to feel our feelings honestly, watch them without judging them, accept everything we have inside, and *choose again for our goal.*

This was exemplified in my story of completing 3,000 bows. I didn't know it at the time, but when I pulled over to the side of the road and was shouting, "What do I really want?" I was evaluating my situation: I faced my feelings of confusion and desperation without judgment, accepted how I felt with surrender, and chose to return home to complete my goal.

When we evaluate, the more specific and measurable the goal is, the better. Because I had a clear goal of 3,000 bows, I had the power to break through my intense emotion, desires, and physical exhaustion to cross the finish line. If I had not had a determined mind to reach the 3,000th bow, when it started to get really hard for me to continue, I would have quit. I would have listened to the voices of my aching body and crazy mind, concluding that, at that late hour, I had done enough for the night, and it was time to go to bed. The motivation to persevere came only from that very clear goal I had set—the promise I had made to myself.

Sometimes, our choices are clear, but our goals are not. Let's say, for example, we decide that instead of choosing our negative thoughts and emotions, we want to choose love, because love is what we feel when we connect with our True Selves. After we choose to love, we need to make loving actions to align ourselves with that choice. However, as we go through our day, trying to be as loving as possible, we discover there are many challenges. Maybe someone we care about says something hurtful, or we get upset about injustices we hear on the news, or suddenly we come down with a headache and just don't feel capable of choosing to love in that condition. This is all very normal. At this point, we wake up to the fact that we need a goal—specific and measurable—to help us manifest our choice to love.

What might be a loving goal? Maybe we decide to call one person a day and share what we love about them, or maybe we choose to look at our own eyes in the mirror when we wake up in the morning and say to ourselves, "I love you," three times in a row, as we feel our hearts. This is goal setting. It doesn't have to be a big goal, it just needs to be something that can be evaluated, something that we can look back on at the end of the day and check to see if we did it or not.

If we didn't do what we said we were going to do, instead of beating ourselves up, we just need to repeat the steps. We need to take time to feel what got in our way, watch and accept that feeling, and choose again to take action for our goal. Based on this thorough evaluation, we can adjust our actions if we need to.

For instance, perhaps we decide that we would prefer to express ourselves in an email to a loved one rather than a phone call. We might decide that saying, "I love you," to our own eyes in the mirror is bringing up too much resistance, so instead, we can begin by writing a list of five things we love about ourselves in a journal each night.

With a specific and measurable goal, we can feel the fulfillment of completion, and our brain begins to tell us, "I can do it. I can do the things I choose." This confidence, this brain power, is important if we are to become creators of our lives.

It's not always comfortable to set a goal, because we tend to fear failure. Consciously or unconsciously, we want to avoid feeling bad, wrong, or not good enough in the face of potential defeat. However, those are limitations we need to break through. The process of breaking through becomes joyful the more we realize that even those limitations are not us, they're ours.

This is a process, of course. All we need to do is practice applying the steps of Self-Mastery over and over again in order to break through our obstacles, until we create what we truly intend.

Sometimes, this takes a long time. For example, I have had the goal of writing this book for more than ten years. However, my mind was full of voices about how I didn't have the time for it, how it wasn't the "right" thing for me to do, or how I couldn't overcome my writer's block whenever I sat down in front of a blank Word document on the computer screen.

I even ignored messages from the universe. In 2016, on a meditation tour in New Zealand, the guide led us to the foot of a massive Hwangchil tree. She told us to close our eyes and sincerely ask the ancient tree a question in our minds. She said that once we opened our eyes, the tree would have a message for us. The question that came to my mind was: *What more do I need to do to contribute to making a better world?* When I opened my eyes and gazed at the immense beauty before me, what I heard, loud and clear, was, "When are you going to write that book, already?" I was shocked. *No, no, it can't be!* I told myself, disregarding what I'd heard. *That must have been my ego, not the tree's message. A Hwangchil tree in the middle of an ancient forest in New Zealand definitely would not talk to me that way.* Yet, the tree's message remained in my heart, pricking and poking me like a splinter, reminding me there was important work to be done.

The Covid-19 pandemic and ensuing lockdown ensured I could no longer ignore the message. For the first time in twenty years, my schedule, like that of so many others, was upended. I sat in my bedroom, unable to run to the center for my next class or appointment. Staring out the window, I thought, *If now is not the opportune time to write my book, I don't know when it will ever be.*

Even though I became clear about what I wanted to do, the old voices came flooding back. This time I decided to face them. I did a lot of Dahn Jon tapping, speaking out all the voices and the fearful, anxious, worrisome emotions that came with them. As I felt them and watched them without judging, I realized they could all be categorized as just one thing: excuses. I finally accepted that my excuses were always going to be there, and I would never be perfectly ready. In spite of them, I made a choice to step forward and begin the project. I took action by copying and pasting every one of my blog posts into a Word document, making a promise to myself to work on this creative endeavor for at least ten minutes a day, no matter what. That was my beginning.

The process has been difficult. When I feel stuck and unclear, when I am uncertain how to break through or what decision to make, or when I don't know where to get the energy and strength for all I need to accomplish, I pause. I feel myself in the moment, watch myself, accept myself, and choose again for the goal of birthing *Healing Tree* and all it means to me. Whenever I need to, I straighten my spine in half-lotus posture, tap my Dahn Jon rhythmically, and speak aloud to myself, "I have the feeling of fear, resistance, worries. These feelings are not me, they're mine. I choose to feel my Dahn Jon. What do I really want for my True Self? What action do I need to take for what I really want?" These sentences open an honest internal conversation and provide loving assistance for me to cross the evaluation bridge on the journey toward my creation. The evaluation process requires a tremendous amount of patience, self-forgiveness, and self-love.

This is step seven—Evaluate.[12]

Recommended Training for Evaluate

Whenever you meet obstacles and struggles on the way to achieving the goals you have set, try this training for yourself:

1.   Tap your Dahn Jon while repeating the following sentences:

---

12   Evaluate is part of Brain Education step #5: Brain Mastering.

"I have the feeling of _____. This feeling is not me, it's mine. I choose to feel my Dahn Jon. What do I really want? What action do I need to take for what I really want?"

2. As you talk it out, allow yourself to feel the choice you are making, the choice to feel your Dahn Jon.

3. As energy comes down to your lower belly, your head will clear, and answers to your questions will arise spontaneously. You don't have to think about them.

4. Keep a notebook nearby so that you can briefly jot down your inspired ideas as you continue the training for twenty minutes.

Create

$\mathcal{S}$elf-Mastery is exactly this: becoming the creator of one's life.

Rather than living as a victim of my external circumstances, of my past, or my future, rather than being a slave to my negative thoughts, emotions or beliefs, I become the master of my life. *I create myself to be the person I truly want to be; I create my life as the life I truly want to live.*

No matter who we are or what conditions we find ourselves in, this is possible. It is possible by mastering our inner world, first. We don't even have to become *masters* of our inner world to experience this creative potential, as that word can sound so elevated and the goal so hard to attain. We need only to practice repeatedly. We need to go within, recognize our cloudy layers, remember that our inner sun is who we really are, and make choices and actions for that self. As this process unfolds, we naturally discover that the power to create is in our hands and can be developed as much as we choose. Creating is simply the result of having a clear idea of what we want to create, taking action on it, and navigating through obstacles successfully.

For years, I have used the Self-Mastery steps daily because I have a dream I want to create. I want to cultivate myself into the greatest version of myself so I can *be* a light in this world.

To this end, I have been healing myself, challenging myself, transforming myself, and awakening myself continuously. I want to share my heart of love with others so they, too, can find and become their inner light. I dream of a world where there are many bright souls shining their love, living in harmony with each other and the earth.

With my dream always in mind, I am motivated to reawaken myself whenever I become disconnected from my body. This dream gives me courage to feel, watch and accept my shadows and suffering, and reminds me that they are not who I really am. This dream inspires me to choose healing actions for myself, to apply them in my interactions with others, and to evaluate myself again and again. This dream encourages me to become the conscious creator of my life.

Despite all the work I was pouring into achieving this dream, about eight years ago, I felt a lack of creatorship in my life. As 2014 came to an end, I looked back, and it all seemed so hazy. Where had the time gone? What had I really done to cultivate myself and my life? I was sure I had done a lot, managing centers, training students, and working on my own self-development; however, there was nothing that clearly stood out to me. It was as if I had become so busy with life that I was unconsciously allowing it to lead me along. It took a lot of Dahn Jon tapping to realize and *accept* that this was happening, but when I finally did, I made a new choice: I would increase my power to create by more consciously designing the direction for my upcoming year. I longed to be the master of my year instead of a slave to it. I declared the year 2015 my year of "new beginnings," and it was! It was the year I birthed my *Healing Tree* blog at daniellegaudette.com.

I felt empowered by the result of my conscious year, so from that time on, I resolved to give each new year a theme. I would take out a journal and begin by stating my title for the upcoming year, then freely listing all that I wanted to work on, change, emphasize, achieve, and add to my life. It was a free-from-judgment list, expressing my honest hopes and dreams, giving me room to stretch my creative wings. Only where I saw fit, I would add in specific and measurable goals that would allow me to get closer to achieving my hopes and dreams but didn't burden me in a way that doused my creative fires. I would end up with a comprehensive list that allowed my heart to soar freely while simultaneously giving me clear action guidelines to evaluate myself.

These lists felt different to me than making New Year's resolutions because they were fail-proof: they were mutable lists that I would continue to look at throughout the year, checking from time to time to see what I had already created and what I needed to keep working on. If I hadn't completed something in a year, and it was still important to me, I would simply add it to the next year's list, without criticizing myself. The purpose of the list was not to make me feel like a failure but to empower me to declare my choices and encourage me to evaluate myself as I embarked on the inspiring challenge of manifesting my design.

As I kept my commitment to this process, refining it continuously as I went along, I found that I began to interpret the year's events as great gifts, teachers, and opportunities that had come into my life to help me achieve that year's theme. I adopted the perspective that the cosmos itself was trying to help me create my life.

For instance, this is from my blog post, dated March of 2020:

Back in December, I chose my 2020 theme. It was "unconditional love." We never know how the universe will twist and turn itself to help us achieve our goals, right?

Standing here at this moment, looking at the world, quarantined in my house, limited in the work I can do, feeling the collective suffering, I keep asking myself, *What should I do? What should I do in this moment for the dream that I live for? What should I do to create a brighter earth and a peaceful humanity?*

I get the same answer every time I ask. Each time it gets louder and clearer: *Love.*

Love and love and keep loving. Love the people your heart was closed to, the people that you felt hurt you, the people far away from you, and the people near you. Just love endlessly and infinitely and let that love make waves and bring your dream back to you like the tide coming in. Love big and wide without expectation of return. Love with your purity, your sincerity, your authenticity, your truth. Love without conditions.

For me, 2020 *was* a year of great love. Since the centers were closed, it seemed more important than ever to move my Self-Mastery classes online, where I was able to continue to give love to my students, supporting them with tools to process their emotions in a time of crisis. I finally had time to begin a project that had been on my create-list since 2015, but was always postponed, a project that has allowed me to grow my self-love—the project of writing my book. I felt more love even in little things, such as the sounds of so many birds tweeting outside my window, the quiet walks through my neighborhood, the friendly smiles from neighbors that spoke without words, *We're all in is this together.*

Most outstanding of all in 2020 was the unexpected way that unconditional love came to me through deep heart-healing. Five old friends, from five different stages of my life, reappeared for reconciliation, like loving gifts from the cosmos. These were people I had unresolved issues with, for one reason or another, issues that had left my heart with unsettled aches. Some of those hurts came from the recent past and some as far back as seventeen years. One by one, my old friends and I reconnected. I bumped into one at an event, two of them texted me out of the blue, one appeared three times in my dreams, so I had no choice but to reach out to him, and the last one finally made herself available for my phone call. Each of them allowed me to put my old hurts to rest, healing my heart with forgiveness and opening the floodgates of unconditional love.

I had never imagined it would happen that way, but those reconciliations, and the gift of unconditional love they brought me, made me feel that a small piece of my bigger dream was coming true: we were co-creating a more loving world.

For a long time, I have wanted to be a Healing Tree of love and light for many other souls who are traveling on their own healing journeys. The work I do at the centers and online, teaching and coaching other instructors and students, my blog posts, and this book are all meant to give back, the way a tree gives back to the forest. I want to be a tree who stands tall and proud, with her arms stretched up to the sky and her roots burrowed deep in the soil, providing whatever she has for the creatures who happen upon her. Recently, a colleague gave me some positive feedback that touched my heart. Not knowing anything about my *Healing Tree* blog or the book, he said, "I learn from your energy that I need to embrace people without judgment so I can become like a tree that people can come to in order to rest, recharge, and refresh their energy when needed."

I aspire to be that tree.

Creating what I want, vibrating together with this creative universe, is the highest level of joy I know—and doing it all for a purpose that is bigger than myself is my greatest privilege.

This is the eighth and final step of Self-Mastery—Create.[13]

Recommended Training for Create

1. Take out your journal. On the top of the page write, **"This Year's Theme: _____"** and fill in the blank. What do you want to create this year? I recommend choosing something general, such as love, trust, or letting go. Let the answer come from your heart. This theme will guide you throughout your year. Even when unexpected things happen, you can interpret them as teachers helping you achieve your goal of trusting more, letting go more.

---

13   Create is part of Brain Education step #5: Brain Mastering.

2. Under your theme, make a list of all the things you'd like to achieve this year. Freely list what you want to work on, change, emphasize, achieve, and add to your life. Let it be a free-from-judgment list, expressing your honest hopes and dreams.

3. Where you see fit, add in goals that are specific and measurable. You might choose, "Meditate at 7:00 a.m. every day," or "Increase my muscle strengthening exercises to four times a week," or "Express my gratitude in my journal at the end of each day."

This list is a guideline for you to practice creating your life. You don't have to be discouraged if after a few weeks, or even months, you haven't accomplished any of the items yet. All you need to do is go back to your journal on a regular basis to check in, see how you're doing, where you're heading, and what you still need to improve. This must be done with no judgment because it can stifle your process. From time to time, make notes about the things you are working on, or are stuck on, and return to Evaluate to help you find your way forward. You can do it!

My Dream

When I was a young girl, I would sit on the kitchen floor, stroking my mother's hair while she, suffering from the intense pain of her own mind, lay her head in my lap. Ever since that time, I have wanted to help people. My compassion began with her in those moments, and as I lived my life, it expanded to all of humanity. From the time I went to college, I opened myself up to feel the pain of our planet. I didn't cry only for the trees, but for the oceans, the skies, and the animals. I yearned for a healthier earth and an awakened humanity.

The moment I realized that Body & Brain had a vision that was in alignment with my deep and desperate wish, I felt hope. It was a big deal, that moment, because hope was something previously missing from my heart. But there it was. For the first time, I felt there was a way that my dream for contributing to this world could somehow be actualized. Until then, I had considered becoming a counselor of sorts, a social worker, or even a teacher; however, none of those satisfied me. I wanted to change myself first.

I wanted to develop myself into a truly bright, loving, healing light for this world. I became intrigued when I was introduced to the Hongik Ingan philosophy—a Korean philosophy that speaks of universal benefit for all humanity. A Hongik Ingan is, to put it simply, a person who lives for the good of all.

I have chosen to become a Hongik Ingan—one who knows that awakening and healing themselves *is* helping others. The only way for me to be truly happy is to awaken, heal, and live a brighter life, and to help others do the same. My choice is to create a win-win situation, one where we all benefit.

For the Good of All
—Ilchi Lee

Regardless of what sort of lives we have lived so far, or what kind of people we believe ourselves to be, we all want to be remembered as people who contributed something to the world.

Somewhere deeper than our victim consciousness, selfishness, and arrogance, somewhere deeper than our instinct to find sensory pleasure, all human beings have a Hongik instinct: we want to do something good for the world.

The Hongik instinct is the fundamental power that caused us to enter the world and the driving force that enables us to keep going, even when weary and troubled. When this Hongik instinct is not fulfilled, we feel somehow empty even after we've finished a busy day's work, and we have regrets about our lives when we end our time in the world.

Somewhere deep in our hearts lives a noble desire to do good for the world. This is the seed of divinity planted deep within us.

Each of us has a dream. And we hope that dream will not stop at the pursuit of our personal profit, but will contribute to our families and neighbors, and, furthermore, to all of society and the human race.

No matter where we work or what kind of jobs we have, no matter whom we work with as we live our lives, deep in our hearts we want to be people who strive to do good for the world. We are originally Hongik Humans.[14]

Even though I dreamed my own version of a Hongik dream before I had ever heard about this Korean philosophy, I wasn't sure that dream could ever be realized. The first flicker of hope came to me during my classes at the center, after I experienced the sensation of ki energy in ji-gam meditation. Each day, as I practiced moving my hands slowly in and out, awakening my sixth sense that quieted my thoughts and lowered my brain waves, I started to feel a lightness about me. I began to shift out of a state of perpetual negativity and into feelings of consistent contentment. As I continued growing that feeling and spending time in a community where this energy is what ties us all together, I began to realize the power of collective consciousness.

One of the principles in Body & Brain is that the stronger energy wins. This means that if I am in a bright and positive mood and walk into a room where there are several angry people, it is highly likely my mood will be affected in a negative way. Conversely, if I am feeling dark and depressed, and I walk into a room of joyful, peaceful, and bright people, my mood will be uplifted. This is the power of energy, the power of the collective.

I had already experienced this power of the collective when I traveled to Korea in June 2001 to attend the New Millennium

14   *Calligraphic Meditation for Everyday Happiness*, Ilchi Lee, Best Life Media, Gilbert, AZ, 2015.

World Peace and Humanity Conference. It was an event set to have 12,000 attendees from all over the world, celebrating love for humanity and love for the earth. Before the event, I had been touring Korea with my fellow Body & Brain practitioners. We had visited mountains, temples, and retreat centers. Everywhere we went, we heard stories about how Korea was facing a serious drought. It was a hot summer, and farmers were struggling because the lack of rain was affecting their rice crops, negatively impacting the livelihood of families and communities throughout the country. Even as I entered the indoor stadium on the day of the event, there was talk all around me about "praying for rain."

Squeezed among so many people that day, I was not feeling very well. On the tour, I had been eating a lot of rice and bulgogi, a popular Korean beef dish, neither of which were part of my usual diet. My intestines were not digesting properly, my stomach ached, and my head was pounding. On top of that, I was feeling agitated because my translation device was sending loud crackling feedback into my ears. There seemed to be a distant voice of broken English mixed in, but I couldn't make out what it was saying. I felt overwhelmed and a bit lost.

There was a lot of commotion as the ceremony was about to begin. Candles and lighters were being passed around for everyone to share. I received my lighter and candle, but when I tried to light it, it wouldn't catch. Panicking, I turned to the person next to me and said, "Help!" He lit my candle and, finally, I was able to look up and see what was going on.

That's when time stood still.

What I saw were 12,000 lights burning in the darkness. I was breathless. I could not see any faces, but I could feel 12,000 souls. I felt a connection to every one of them. There we were, lights from all over the world, honoring the same dream for humanity and the earth, all at the same time.

Above the stage, a large banner hung with an image of Mother Earth, surrounded by her blue aura, floating in space. I gazed at her magnificence. As I did, I felt waves of energy cascading over me, huge waves of energy filled with deep love and reverence for humanity and the earth. I was not "praying" per se; praying was just happening to me. In my mind, I saw an image of the 12,000 of us as souls in outer space before we came to the earth, gathered around this precious planet. We were calling out desperately, with the compassion of loving children, feeling the pain of our Mother, and declaring our promise to come to the rescue.

"Mom! Mom! We will help you!"

Tears poured down my face as my heart opened wide. I felt a sense of mission like I'd never felt before. I felt responsibility and, at the same time, genuine hope.

I turned to the people next to me, and they, too, were weeping—and laughing. We carefully doused our candles and began to hug each other. We hugged and smiled the purest and most holy smiles at one another. The entire stadium was doing the same. It seemed we were all feeling something beyond words that only our hearts understood: 12,000 hearts dreaming the same dream at the same moment, 12,000 prayers, 12,000 lights for the world.

In an instant, the stadium exploded into a celebration of

light and sound. Festive music reverberated wall to wall, and confetti showered us from the ceiling, as giant earth beach balls bounced throughout the audience. The presenters were clapping and dancing. Even Ilchi Lee was spinning across the stage like a pinwheel.

We dashed toward the stage to join in long dance trains with strangers from different countries. We were making new friends, taking group photos, and crying in each other's arms. It was as if the earth herself was celebrating with us. I felt her great joy and love as she witnessed her children becoming one.

The dancing and laughter continued, even as we were being ushered out into the streets where, to our surprise, we discovered it had begun to rain!

We cheered in the streets, collectively feeling that all our love and joy had opened the skies. The drought had come to an end!

Did we make it rain? I'm not sure if such a thing could be proven. But it certainly felt that heaven and earth were moved by the massive explosion of energy that I witnessed in the stadium that day. I choose to believe that this was the result of our collective consciousness. There was a critical mass—a single wish held deeply in the hearts of so many people at one time that it had a multiplying effect. It had moved beyond us, interacting with nature itself.

If human beings could raise their individual consciousness levels to become more awake, more aware, more connected to themselves and all living things—more Hongik—and gather into a critical mass, our world problems would naturally be solved, one by one. Once I had experienced the powerful potential of critical mass, I wanted to participate in lifting up the collective consciousness of the earth, together with my fellow Earth Citizens. What is an Earth Citizen? I think Ilchi Lee's "Earth Citizen Declaration" says it best. I share it here, as it contains my vision, my dream, and my aspiration.

Earth Citizen Declaration

I declare that I am an Earth Citizen who loves and cherishes all humans and all life, as someone who has found my value and recovered my character.

I declare that I am an Earth Citizen who contributes to making a happy, healthy family and peaceful community.

I declare that I am an Earth Citizen who lives for an Earth Village where all humanity lives as one family beyond nationality, race and religion.

I declare that I am an Earth Citizen who acts to protect and restore the global ecosystem so that the earth may recover its original beauty and vitality.

I declare that I am an Earth Citizen who takes part in the work of developing one hundred million Earth Citizens for the evolution of human consciousness and the advent of a new era of civilization on earth.

Some days, I finish my morning meditation by making this declaration out loud. As I speak each word, I imagine people all over the world, declaring themselves as Earth Citizens, living in accordance with the message and spirit that the declaration contains.

This hope lives in my heart, and though it may seem naive, I believe it can happen. In fact, I believe it *is* happening. It may not always look that way, but during times of transformation, things often get worse before they get better. That is part of the purification process. The old, unhealthy consciousness is being cleansed, making way for a newer, brighter, more awakened consciousness to become manifest.

There's nothing we can't do, if only we choose to do it. We need a critical mass of people choosing to become brighter, more harmonious contributors to the planet, people choosing to create loving and peaceful environments within themselves and all around them. When enough of these people gather, consciousness will jump and change will happen. It is said that when about one hundred million people across the world create such a consciousness, the shift will take place.

I have decided to be one of them.

Kate's Womb Revisited

It's been twenty-two years since I've had Kate in my life. Our relationship holds a sensitive place in my heart. With her, it's a short distance to feeling a huge kind of healing that comes when I finally have a ground to stand on, a wall to lean against. Yet, it is also a short distance to feeling a kind of hurt that no one else has the power to trigger in quite the same way. Therein lies the mini-minefield that I am always navigating when we see each other.

I have come a long way. Through Body & Brain and the steps of Self-Mastery, through living for my dream, I have slowly processed the shock of my primal wound. I have discovered, undoubtedly, that in the end, I never want to hurt Kate, and I feel that she doesn't want to hurt me either. I love her, and I believe she loves me. It has taken me a lot of practice and perseverance, moving through impossibly confusing and painful feelings, to finally realize that we each have our own perspectives. We each have our own lives, our own stories, memories, and wounds hiding within us that don't always allow the love we have inside to be made manifest. The more I come to accept my perspectives, stories, memories, and wounds, the more I accept hers. Judgment then turns into compassion, and healing energy flows between us.

Our relationship is still a work in progress, a work of art

that's being created choice by choice, time after time. In my most enlightened moments, I like to focus on the essence, the deepest root of our connection.

Once, during a special training, I experienced this connection. We were being led into a process of healing, focusing on our belly buttons—the precious place in our bodies where we have nerve endings that still remember our connection to our mother's womb. We did a lot of massaging inside the belly button as well as on the acupressure points around it to loosen the tension in our organs. Then, we were taken into a deep meditation.

We were guided to breathe in and out through our belly buttons and receive the energy of the cosmos. As I breathed, the earth appeared, floating in space in front of me. She was surrounded by a field of golden light. Her luminous aura formed a funnel, pouring directly into my belly button, filling me with loving light.

The trainer then instructed us to follow the feeling of connection from our belly button, through our energetic umbilical cord, to our mother's womb. As I focused, I was catapulted back to that place.

Inside Kate's womb, rather than feeling warm and cozy, I felt myself bombarded by angst and confusion, sadness and fear. It was like being in a dark, loud cave where I had to tense my whole body to protect myself from the incredibly noisy emotion. It was a familiar feeling—an uncomfortable, victimized feeling that often surfaced when I would go deep within.

This time, however, a message came to me. The message was from Mother Earth. She told me, "Although you received pain in Kate's womb, you also received the force of Life. Feel the golden Life that you received from your mother who birthed you."

Suddenly, I could feel it—pure, sparkling, hot Life—flowing like lava from my mother's body into mine via the umbilical cord that had once joined us. Inside that pure Life, my tension dissolved. My angst, my victimized feelings disintegrated. The hurt, the pain could not survive; it simply could not exist inside the colossal current of the unconditional love I felt.

Deep gratitude for Kate came pouring out of my heart. It was a gratitude I had never felt before—a gratitude not only for being grown inside of Kate's womb, but also for being *created* there, for being made from her very blood and bones. I was a part of Kate's body, and we shared the very Life that coursed through both of us.

Bathed inside this sacred knowing, riding the rhythm of my breathing, I came to understand the profound meaning of belly-button healing. It was a healing that went far beyond physical health benefits; it was a spiritual healing of the oldest memory of my nerves and cells, a healing of my deepest wound, a healing that was medicine for my soul.

As an adoptee trying to heal this primal wound, I realized how critical it is to take time to recognize the pure Life I received from the one who grew me inside her. That Life does not belong to me, nor does it belong to my birth mother; it is Life itself, the Life that animates this entire cosmos. It is the gift—the great and mysterious sacred gift—that transcends the "good and bad" phenomena of this human existence. It is the immeasurable gift that I received inside of Kate's womb.

I Am Ready

I n honor of the Life we both share, I've decided the time to write my healing letter to Kate is now. It has taken me nearly twenty years to prepare myself. Only after meeting with the essence of our connection, only after looking into the deep corners of my heart over and over, only after writing this book, am I finally clear about what I really want to say.

Here and now, on this day in 2021, my year of "Trust," I am ready to write this letter.

Dear Kate,

I'm sorry. I'm sorry that it's been so hard for us. I'm sorry for every moment of pain that you must have endured. I'm truly sorry. I'm sorry for all the hurts of the past, even of other lifetimes—who knows? I'm sorry. For all of my anger and blame, my lack of gratitude, my complaints, my self-victimization, I'm sorry.

I hope you will forgive me, Kate. Forgive me for being complicated. Whether it is from being given up for adoption, or from being raised by someone who suffered with mental illness, or because I was born with a moon in Scorpio—or all of the above—I know that I am truly complex. Please forgive me for my lack of compassion, my disrespect, and my insistence on suffering for so many years. I have probably caused you even more pain than you had already experienced. Forgive me that my healing process has taken longer than I had hoped. Forgive me.

Thank you, Kate. Thank you for birthing me. I appreciate you for making the hard choice to bring me to this planet. And thank you for finding me. So many adoptees never get the chance to meet their birth mothers. I feel grateful to have met you and to have had time to heal with you. I know this could only have happened because of your courage, your determination, and your tenacity. I'd like to hope I have inherited some of those qualities from you. For all of this, I am so very thankful.

I love you, Kate. I do. I didn't feel it at the beginning. The place in my heart where you existed was numbed over at first with some kind of protective painkiller. There was great resistance. Cynicism. It took a while, but as I allowed that anesthesia to wear off, to my surprise, there was a bright sunburst of love that had been there all along. It felt so good to find it. Finally, I could breathe, knowing I had made something right inside. Finally, I could love my mother who created me, who brought me into this world with literal blood, sweat, and tears. It feels so good to love you, Kate. I am happy to have the chance to know you and to love you in this lifetime.

Your daughter,
Danielle

I Have Me

O ver the past two decades, I've come to discover that my bright soul has been slowly seeping its light into every aspect of my life. It's as if my experience at the Finding True Self workshop provided only a sneak preview of my possibility. My journey has been a "becoming."

For me, the realization is to never give up. It's a message that transformation takes time. It's incremental. It requires a great deal of steadfast discipline, devotion, patience, self-forgiveness, and love.

I have always wished that suddenly, one day, *boom!* I would be fully awake. That wish has left me frustrated and disappointed with myself so many times. I am learning through living that I need to take a good, honest look at all the desires and expectations my ego has put in my path. Then, I can accept that it was just my perception, my own egoic lens, that was causing so much suffering.

I have heard Ilchi Lee say that "suddenly one day" comes after a long period of effort and devotion. What I take from that perspective is that there is no "suddenly one day." Everything in this universe is a fair trade. What we put in is what we get out. Therefore, what is truly important is our devotion—our endless attention to our growth and transformation, our willingness to share and apply each truth that blossoms along the way.

This is the beauty of the journey. Just as the mountain is made up of many grains of sand, out of our mighty efforts, "suddenly one day" something great will be born.

In 2020, I celebrated my twentieth year of practicing Body & Brain. I am proud of myself that, through all the hardships and struggles I have experienced over the last twenty years, I have been able to hold on to my truth. I have been able to maintain the choice I made for my soul at the time—to honor and protect the light I had found and to live my life dedicated to it.

It didn't make sense to some people around me that I was so committed to something not seen by the physical eye nor valued by this material world. But my spiritual sense had awakened, and from that view, there was only one thing to do—to live for something bigger than my small self, to choose for something greater than my small life.

I met my soul and chose my path, but changing negative habits takes a lifetime. Perhaps my most severe habit of all was that I could not recognize my own self-worth.

Little by little, day by day, practice after practice, a knowing came to me:

Every star in the sky is beautiful. Every blade of grass is beautiful. Every single flower, no matter how small or big, growing in a garden or in the wild, with all its uniqueness, deformations, colors and shapes, adored by many or never once seen by a human eye, is, in fact, truly beautiful. Every single one of them. And I, too, am like those stars that sparkle in the night sky. I, too, am like those blades of green grass, so small yet so powerful, withstanding the wind and rain. I, too, am a beautiful flower—living among all the other beautiful flowers of humanity—here on planet Earth.

No one can ever take this away from me—no matter who keeps me or gives me away, no matter who loves me madly or rejects me deeply, no matter who wins or who loses, who succeeds or who fails. No one can ever take my true nature away from me.

This single knowing has been my greatest healing of all.

I wish to thank you who have come to the end of my story for partaking in the Healing Tree. I hope you have received some nutrients for your own soul to nourish you on your journey.

If I have a final message, it is this: Recognize yourself. Recognize the pure and beautiful soul that you are. Only you can do that for yourself, and you can choose to do it anytime, anywhere. You are valuable and whole, in and of yourself, always. Shine your light. Every single light is so precious and so important at this moment in time. A brighter world is waiting for us.

Resources

Danielle Gaudette, daniellegaudette.com

Sedona Mago Center for Well-Being and Retreat, sedonamagoretreat.org

Body & Brain Yoga and Tai Chi, bodynbrain.com or youtube.com/bodynbrain

Finding True Self Workshop, sites.google.com/bodynbrain. com/workshops/beginner/finding-true-self

Brain Education, youtube.com/braineducationtv

Self-Mastery, daniellegaudette.com or Emotional Self-Mastery series, youtube.com/bodynbrain

Ilchi Lee, ilchi.com or youtube.com/ilchilee

Acknowledgments

From its first bud of an idea to its full flowering, *Healing Tree* has been a ten-year journey. As I come to the end of this growth process, I recognize there are precious people who helped me make this creation possible. With all my heart, I'd like to acknowledge them here.

Foremost among them is my beloved writing coach, Bonnie Taschler. There are no words or gestures big enough to describe the gratitude I have for the time and sincerity she so generously donated to me. It is not an understatement to say I could not have made this dream a reality without her. Along with all she has taught me about the art of writing, her steadfast support, encouragement, and belief in the message of *Healing Tree* lifted me up, time and again. She was the only one who listened to *all* my stories, hopes, ideas, and woes with loving patience and sincere consideration. Her immense kindness has been one of my greatest blessings.

I also want to thank the beautiful people from kn literary arts: Christina Thiele, who helped me realize my vision for the cover and interior design; Helen Burroughs, who assisted with the proofreading; Nirmala Nataraj, who did my developmental edit, helping me flesh out important concepts more thoroughly and organize the book in a way I couldn't see how to do by myself; and Elisabeth Rinaldi, who became my "midwife," kindly walking me through the final steps of my book-birthing process.

I want to thank Michael Starace, Ben Levit, Mia Muratori, and my birth mother, Kate Mulgrew—dear ones who allowed me to read selected pieces to them early on. Their loving feedback helped shape certain descriptive parts of the memoir.

For all the little but so important things, I want to express my appreciation to Christie Jensen and Sachi Maekawa, two lovely ladies who patiently attended to all my "please help me's."

I'd like to give a big shout-out to the generous people who contributed to my GoFundMe campaign. They made it possible for me to raise enough money for this project! Thank you so much to: Pam Myers, Jesse Martinsen, Paul Liebert, Charlene Dazols, Renée Gaudette, Ginger Chaffin, Upama Barua, Bob Gaudette, Bobby Lynn, Robert Herbst, Helen David, Gail Manzelli, Judy Campbell, Pamela Vecchione, Jeanie Gaskill, Barbara Batchelor, Anne Bush, Manon Brinkman, Arthur Bergeron, Judy O'Neil, Elaine Canina, Michael Starace, John Taylor, Russell Hammond, Kerry Evans, Melissa Penny, Linda Burnett, Alexis McKinney, Claudia van Wijnen, Vinson Shinabery, Catharine Koenheim, Darlene Hermes, Cindy Mitrano, Dorothy Finer, Carol LaPlante, Edward Gaudette, Maki Perry, Janice Martin, Julie Tizard, Robin Blake, Stephanie Stabile, Sherry Johnson, Bennett Levit, Amy Anderson, Barbara Sek, Carolyn Moore, Erin Gruber, Arthur Babakhanov, Lisa Garabedian, Robin Glazebrook, Leeta Aulet, Maryanne Bardsley, Jeff Nielson, Bruce Levy, Marc Manzelli, Young Park, and Virginia Causey. Special thanks to Charles Burnett, Chun Kwang, and Leslie Ray, and an extra special thanks to Phil Erickson. Every donation filled me with hope and powered me forward through my challenging moments.

My heartfelt gratitude and deep love go out to some of the "main characters" in my life who made this memoir what it is:

My beloved father, Robert Gaudette, the rock of my life, one of the purest, kindest, most giving souls I have ever known. He cheered me on every step of the way and touched my heart with his effort to generously fundraise for me among family and friends. My father's love for me has always been unconditional—I am who I am because of his quiet, consistent, unwavering, supportive presence in my life.

My biological mother, Kate Mulgrew, for giving me her blessing to tell our story as seen through the eyes of my own heart. I know it's not easy for her to hear about my suffering, yet she has bravely encouraged me to tell my truth. As one who shares my passion to express, create, and write, she has been fully understanding of my process. Her support for this book has been particularly meaningful to me because, as I have already said, it gives me ground to stand on and a wall to lean against. Her openness and generosity have been a testament to her love, and I am so thankful. I have found the writing of our story to be healing for me, and I can only hope it has offered the same gift to her.

My sister, Renée Gaudette, who praised my decision to write this book and the effort it took to complete it. Though it's easy for the relationships of youth to weaken over time, I am grateful that she and I have grown closer with each passing year. With our mother gone, we work hard to take care of each other, and having her love and support in my adult life is precious to me.

As the book itself shows, I am grateful for the existence of Body & Brain and for the people who have supported me in my growth along the way. I want to especially thank my team here in Washington State: Yang Je Chon, my manager, for allowing me to take the time I needed to do this project, as well as Hyo Jung Im, Maki Perry, Melanie Kreischer, Diep Mai, and Crispina Talens, my center managers and assistants, who worked to care for the members and keep the centers alive and online during the difficult time of the Covid-19 pandemic. My trust in them permitted me the time to see this book through to the end.

During their wildly busy schedules, Jiyoung Oh from Best Life Media and David Driscoll from Body & Brain made time to meet my needs and help me move forward. Similarly, Jordan Diamond accommodated my last-minute need for a photo shoot, producing my back cover bio picture. Receiving their support eased my heart and put wind in my sail.

It was the current CEO of Body & Brain, Oceana, my original mentor, from whom I learned the eight steps of Self-Mastery. Her mentorship came at a critical time of my life, bringing awakenings, healing, and growth. For all the love and care she provided, I thank her from the bottom of my heart.

Finally, I want to thank my teacher, Ilchi Lee, who, when all I saw was darkness in the world, showed me that great light, enormous love, and tremendous hope lived within me. To express the depth of my gratitude, I continue to heal myself, to deepen my connection to who I truly am, and to share my light.

About the Author

Danielle Gaudette has been writing poetry and short stories since she was six years old. She graduated from the University of Iowa where she continued her study of creative writing. Her *Healing Tree* blog can be found at daniellegaudette.com.

After finding her True Self in 2000, she took time to explore her inner world and worked to help others do the same. As a twenty-year trainer and coach in Body & Brain principles and practices, she currently works in Seattle as the regional director of Washington Body & Brain Centers.

She cares deeply about honesty, transparency, and making sure people feel safe, encouraged, and empowered to go within themselves to face their pain and hardships. She believes that in doing so they will be able to uncover the strength and wisdom to heal their inner wounds and create themselves anew.

This is how she lives her life: she practices facing her own wounds and has found that, in doing so, she is brought closer to her True Self. She shares her story in *Healing Tree* to help others find the courage to go inward, the courage to heal their hearts.

Her passion is to continue to awaken herself to the true principles of the universe and to help others awaken as well.

She feels that with every person who chooses to do their own inner work, we are lifting the collective heaviness, fear, resentment, and darkness, and we are brightening humanity—together.